Seeds of Grace

Introducing Young Hearts to Sin and Salvation through the King James Bible

By

Gary E. Risenhoover

Published by Kinetic Digital Publishers

www.kineticdigitalpublishers.com

For permissions, inquiries, or other correspondence, please visit our website.

ISBN eBook: 979-8-90235-114-6
ISBN Paperback: 979-8-90235-115-3
ISBN Hardcover: 979-8-90235-116-0
LCCN: 2026908899

TABLE OF CONTENTS

Preface

Dearest little reader, and beloved guardian who holds this book close, welcome to a journey that is both ancient and ever new, a journey where the whispers of the ages unfold like petals in a dawn-lit garden, inviting us to wander together through the sacred landscapes of sin and salvation, kindness and grace. It is with profound joy and tender hope that I present to you *Seeds of Grace*, a humble offering crafted to nurture young hearts by introducing them to the gentle majesty of the King James Bible and the everlasting truths it holds. In these pages, the timeless words of scripture are woven with care into stories and reflections designed to speak softly to the imaginations and spirits of children, guiding them gently into the warm embrace of God's love.

The world is a vast and wondrous place, filled with beauty beyond measure and mysteries that stir the soul. Yet even amidst the light, shadows fall, and the tender hearts of children must begin to understand the delicate balance between joy and sorrow, innocence and experience, right and wrong. It is here in this sacred tension that *Seeds of Grace* takes root; here we explore the profound themes of sin and redemption, not as distant or frightening concepts, but as invitations to grow, to learn, to forgive, and to hope. This book aims to cradle young minds with stories that echo the rhythms of the King James Bible's poetic language, stories that spark curiosity and empathy, and lessons that transform ancient teachings into vibrant, tender truths accessible to the smallest ears and newest hearts.

From the earliest stirrings of creation, where God's breath painted the heavens and shaped the earth with profound love, we begin with wonder and innocence, a reminder that all was made good. Through the story of

Adam and Eve, those first beloved children of God, we meet the first choice that stirred the course of human life and learn, gently and with great care, about the nature of sin. It is not spoken of here as a heavy burden or an unyielding condemnation, but rather as a breaking of harmony, a moment of misunderstanding amid the vastness of divine love. With warmth and openness, young readers are invited to see that sin touches everyone yet is never the last word, for the story continues into the realms of mercy and salvation.

As the chapters unfold, the narrative blooms into tales of kindness, repentance, and transformation. Children walk alongside figures who falter and fall, but who rise again through forgiveness, the greatest gift given freely from the hand of God. Central to this hope is the loving figure of Jesus Christ, whose grace flows like living water, washing clean the stains of error and despair. Here, in the gentle embrace of the Savior's story, children discover that no matter how lost one may feel, the light of redemption shines ever bright, guiding souls back to peace. This message is whispered with reverence, echoed in the cadence of scripture's sacred tongue, inviting children not only to hear but to feel the heartbeat of salvation pulsing with eternal strength.

But *Seeds of Grace* is more than a telling of ancient truths; it is a tender companion to the moral awakening of young lives. With each page, it encourages the reader to reflect, to pray, and to dream, to see kindness as a daily beacon and grace as a living force in their world. In transforming complex theology into simple, vivid stories, it plants the seeds of faith, hope, and love within the very soil of a child's heart. These seeds, once nurtured by understanding and care, will grow branches of generosity, leaves of forgiveness, and flowers of unshakeable joy and peace. It is my heartfelt prayer that this book will become a cherished touchstone for families and caregivers, a gentle guidepost on the path toward spiritual growth and everlasting connection with God.

The language of the King James Bible, so rich, so resonant, fills these pages not merely as decoration but as a living voice, breathing old truths into modern ears. Its poetic cadence invites children to experience scripture not as dry doctrine, but as a melody of faith, a song of love, simple yet profound. By introducing this sacred tongue alongside tender explanations, I hope to foster not only understanding but a deep appreciation for the beauty and power of biblical language. It is a language that has carried the hopes and dreams of countless generations, and now it rests within your hands, ready to inspire new hearts with its eternal message.

To the parents, caregivers, and teachers who will share these pages with the children they love, I offer thanks and encouragement. Your role cannot be overstated, for you are the gardeners tending these seeds of grace, watering them with patience, tending them with prayer, and watching with joy as they blossom in faith. May this book serve as a gentle tool in your hands, a spark to ignite conversations about life's deepest questions, a mirror reflecting God's love back into young eyes, and a bridge connecting tender hearts with the everlasting promises written in holy scripture.

As you turn these pages, may you each find comfort in the knowledge that you are not alone on this journey. The sun rises faithfully each day, just as God's grace rises within us, unwavering and warm. Whether you are a child stepping for the first time into the mysteries of faith, or a guide leading a beloved soul along the sacred path, may *Seeds of Grace* be a lamp unto your feet, a beacon of hope, a garden of stories, and an invitation to live with kindness, courage, and joy.

With a heart full of love and a spirit eager to share God's wonderful news, I invite you now to embark upon this tender journey. May these seeds find fertile soil in your heart and bloom into a lifelong understanding of the boundless grace that surrounds us all.

Gary E. Risenhoover

The Garden of Beginnings

In the Beginning

In the beginning, before the sun had kissed the earth with warmth or the moon had begun to drift softly across the sky, there was a vast, deep silence. The world was not yet made, only a darkness stretched wide and still, wrapped in the hush of a gentle quiet that held a promise yet unseen. But then, into that deep and endless quiet, came a voice, a voice gentle yet full of power, speaking words that would bring forth life and light. "Let there be light," the voice said, and in a wondrous moment, light blossomed like a great golden dawn, pushing back the shadows and making the world bright and new.

The light was not glowing from any fire or lamp, but from the very breath of God, shining pure and clear, soft as a morning song and strong as the first awakening of the day. It painted the sky with the promise of morning and evening, a dance of gold and blue and soft pink hues that filled the heart with peace and joy. This light was a special gift, the first beginning of everything that would ever be, bringing warmth, color, and life to a world that had before been quiet and unseen. The light and the darkness were friends in the great song of creation, each having its time and place, each making the other more beautiful.

After the light filled the world, another wondrous thing happened: the voice called forth the sky, a wide, sparkling blue that stretched out like a great, gentle blanket covering the earth. This sky was not just empty air but a grand, spacious home for the clouds, the birds, and all the soft breezes that would someday carry laughter and whisper secrets to the trees. It was high and wide and endless, full of dreams waiting to be heard, a place where the sun would travel each day and the stars would twinkle in the hush of night. This sky made the world feel open and free, inviting all who would look upward to wonder at its beauty and trust in its vastness.

Beneath this sky, the voice called the waters to gather and the dry land to appear, land that would be firm and gentle, strong enough to hold trees and flowers and creatures of every shape and size. The land was soft with grass and rich with the promise of seeds and fruits, a beautiful home fashioned by tender hands for all that was to come. It rose softly from the waters like a cradle, a place where life would dance and grow, where children would someday run and play beneath the sky's wide embrace. The rivers sang their beginning songs as they flowed freely, sparkling in the new light, and the mountains stood tall and proud, guarding the earth with quiet strength.

On this freshly formed earth, everything was bathed in perfect harmony. The light touched every blade of grass and every leaf, sparkling like countless tiny stars fallen onto the world. The sky sang its quiet songs through the rustling trees and across the shimmering lakes. The air held the sweet scent of earth and water mingled, fresh and full of wonder. In this world, nothing was broken or sad; all was good and whole, a beautiful gift made out of love and care. This was a world made to hold laughter and joy, a world ready to welcome all the living things that would soon fill it.

The voice that spoke it all was full of kindness, creating not with hurry or noise, but with slow and patient grace, each step a gentle unfolding of goodness. The light was given to chase away fear, the sky given to remind all creatures of endless possibility, and the land given to cradle the tiny and the great alike in its loving hold. Looking at this creation is like seeing a tender masterpiece, painted not with hurried strokes but with thoughtful, loving hands, as if to say that every small thing in this world matters deeply and is held in a great, joyful purpose.

This beginning is not just a story of things made, it is a story of love that is always making, breathing life into all that is beautiful. It invites young hearts to look around at the wonders in the flowers, the birdsong, the dance of sunlight on water, and know that there is goodness at the root of it all. God's voice, so full of warmth and majesty, calls each child to trust in this world made for joy, to see the world as a garden of hope and light. As the light filled the darkness, so does God fill every heart with a quiet and shining peace, reminding all that, from the very beginning, life is wrapped in grace and endless possibility.

Animals and Plants

In the beginning, when God had fashioned the heavens and the earth, He adorned this new world with an abundant splendor that no eye had yet beheld. As the early morning dew sparkled upon the tender blades of grass, a symphony of life stirred softly beneath the warm breath of the sun. Picture, if you will, a great garden filled with endless wonders, each creature peculiarly fashioned and each plant gloriously unique, knit together in harmonious beauty by the hand of the Almighty. From the tallest trees reaching up as if to whisper secrets to the clouds, to the tiniest flowers tucked quietly among the grasses, all were crafted with a purpose and tender loving care. This garden was not merely a place of green and gold; it was a living canvas of God's creativity, where colors, shapes, and sounds intertwined like the gentle notes of a lullaby sung upon the winds.

Imagine the animals, great and small, each arriving in their perfect beauty to fill the garden with life and joy. The lion, strong and proud, with a mane bright as the morning sun, roamed gracefully through the tall grasses, his powerful roar a majestic song that echoed across the hills. Nearby, the gentle deer bounded lightly among the trees, their eyes soft and trusting, reflecting the peace that dwelled within this sacred place. Frolicsome rabbits hopped between the colorful wildflowers, their noses twitching at the sweet perfumes carried upon the breeze. Above them, the birds glided through the azure sky, their feathers painted in hues dazzling and bright. The lark's melodious song rose clear and pure, announcing the glory of the waking day, while the dove's soft cooing spoke quietly of peace and hope. Each bird's winged flight was a dance, a joyful celebration of the freedom and beauty bestowed by the Creator.

Beneath the leaves and within the burrows, insects hummed their gentle tunes; bees buzzed industriously, gathering nectar from blossoms of every conceivable color, scarlet, violet, gold, and white, each flower carefully fashioned to delight the eye and provide sustenance. The butterflies, with their delicate wings patterned like stained-glass windows, flitted gracefully from bloom to bloom, their dance as gentle as a whisper upon the air. Every creature, whether mighty or minuscule, was a testament to God's boundless imagination, set to live in peace and to praise their Maker in their own wonderful ways.

And the plants! Ah, the plants, how wondrous and varied they were! Towering cedars stood firm and proud, their branches stretched wide to embrace the heavens, while fragrant pines filled the air with the rich smell of evergreen. The delicate lilies, pure and glowing, swayed lightly in the breeze like soft lanterns of the night, illuminating the earth with their humble grace. Grapevines twisted their tendrils with eager fingers, promising sweet fruit that would nourish and delight those who would one day dwell near them. The verdant ferns curled and uncurled like the gentle waves upon a still lake, soft and inviting to the touch. Everywhere the eye rested, there was a marvel to behold: blossoms burst forth in vivid colors, leaves shimmered with a thousand shades of green, and fruits hung heavy and ripe beneath the sun's warm caress, ready to be gathered in the fullness of time.

This garden was a sanctuary of harmony where every living thing was given a place, a purpose, and a song. The balance was perfect; even the rivers and streams, clear as crystal, wound their way through meadows and groves, nourishing roots and quenching the thirst of every creature. The water sparkled in the sun, singing over smooth stones and whispering secrets to the reeds that danced along the banks. The gentle breeze, like a soft breath from God Himself, carried the mingled scents of earth and blossom, the songs of birds, and the laughter of hidden brooks, weaving all things together in a tender embrace of life.

In this wondrous world, light itself seemed to rejoice. The first dawn cast its golden beams across the fertile soil, awakening the colors and the scents, the sounds and the movements. Light shimmered through the canopy, dappling the ground below with patterns of shadow and sun, revealing the delicate lace of leaves and the bright jewels of dew. Day by day, this radiant gift bathed the animals and plants alike, nurturing them with warmth and inviting them into the dance of life. Night, too, was given its own gentle beauty. When the sun slipped below the horizon, the sky became a velvet curtain studded with stars, each one a twinkling testament to God's glory and care, illuminating the peaceful rest of all who dwelt in the garden in quiet assurance and sweet dreams.

Within this sanctuary of creation, every leaf and every feather, every ripple and every petal told a story, a story of love and intention, of goodness and grace. The animals, free from fear or hunger, lived in pure contentment. The plants, rooted firmly in the rich earth, stretched upward and outward, flourishing beneath the watchful gaze of their Creator. This harmony was not merely the absence of strife; it was fullness of peace, the kind that settles deep within the heart and sings softly of belonging. The garden was a place where the voice of God could be heard in the rustle of the leaves and the murmur of the waters, a voice of gentle invitation to delight in all that was good and beautiful and true.

As we close our eyes and imagine ourselves wandering through this garden, it is good to remember that it was not just a place of exquisite beauty but a home, tenderly made for the first humans, Adam and Eve. For them, and for all who would come after, the creatures and plants were to be companions and helpers, teachers and friends. The dove brought messages of peace, the lion taught courage, the trees whispered wisdom through their silent strength, and the flowers shared quiet reminders of gentleness and color amid the green. Everything in the garden worked together in splendid unity, a reflection of the loving heart of God who had made it all. How wondrous it is to know that such a garden was placed at the very beginning of the story, so that we might understand the beauty and goodness that was meant for us from the start, a world where life bloomed richly and freely, where every living thing was cherished and cared for as a precious part of God's grand design.

So, when we look about us, in gardens, in parks, in the wild places under the sun, let us remember this first garden, the grand tapestry woven by God's own hands. Each leaf we see, each bird's song we hear, and each flower's bloom is a gentle echo of the wonder that was here at the beginning. In this, we find a seed of gratitude planted deep within our hearts, a whisper of awe that reminds us how deeply we are loved, how carefully we are cared for, and how we, too, are called to cherish and protect all the beautiful life that surrounds us. For every creature, every tree, and every blooming flower is a letter in God's loving story, written with care so that we might learn the song of grace that begins with the simple, beautiful things made good at the dawn of creation.

Man and Woman

In the beginning, when the world was freshly made and the morning stars sang together, God saw that all He had created was good, very good indeed. The earth blossomed with green grass and tall trees that reached toward the sun like children stretching their hands to hold a warm and loving embrace. The air was sweet with the song of birds, and rivers ran like silver ribbons, chasing one another through fields and valleys. In this perfect world, every creature, from the tiniest ant crawling upon a leaf to the great lions basking under the shade, lived in harmony, each one playing its part in the grand orchestra of life. Yet, even amidst this marvelous beauty and bustling life, something wondrous was about to happen, something that would fill the earth with a special kind of care and kindness unlike any other: the creation of man and woman.

God did not simply make the world and leave it to wander on its own. No, with great love and wisdom, He shaped the first man, Adam, from the dust of the ground. Just as an artist puts every stroke of a brush with purpose and gentle hands, so God breathed life into Adam's form, making him alive and special above all creatures. Adam was not just another part of creation; he was set apart to be the caretaker of God's beautiful world. His eyes, wide and wondering, opened to behold the marvels that God had prepared, the shimmering trees, the radiant skies, and the countless animals that would soon become his friends and companions. But God knew that even this wondrous man needed a helper who would walk beside him, sharing in the stewardship of this perfect garden.

From the same sacred earth that had formed Adam, the Lord took a deep and precious rib and fashioned for him a woman, Eve, full of kindness and grace. She was not made to be lesser or weak, but to be a companion, a partner who would work together in love and harmony with Adam. Together, man and woman were given a glorious place in the midst of creation, the garden called Eden, a playground of beauty where rivers flowed from springs like crystal and every tree bore fruit of dazzling colors and sweet perfume. In this haven, Adam and Eve were more than visitors; they were gardeners, caretakers appointed by the Creator Himself to nurture and protect the life surrounding them.

The specialness of man and woman was not found in their strength or in their size but in the tender responsibility given to them. God entrusted them to name the animals, teaching them the languages of creation as a way to understand and appreciate each creature's unique role. This naming was more than just words; it was an act of love, a way to draw closer and care for all that God had painted with infinite detail. In their innocence, Adam and Eve walked hand in hand beneath dazzling skies, their faces glowing with the light of a world perfect and unbroken. They smelled the fresh fragrance of blooming flowers and listened to the gentle rustle of leaves, their hearts full of wonder at the artistry of God's design.

As caretakers, they were given joy, but also a gentle task to tend the garden wisely. They were like tiny gardeners turning soft earth and planting seeds, making sure every vibrant plant and playful creature grew safe and strong. Every day was filled with discovery and gratitude, a dance of life in harmony with the divine heartbeat that pulsed through the earth, the sky, and every living thing. This was a time without sorrow, where curiosity and kindness bloomed freely within the garden's walls. Adam and Eve learned the secret language of creation, feeling each leaf's quiver and each animal's whisper, as if the entire garden breathed alongside them in shared joy.

Yet, even more special than their role was the close friendship Adam and Eve shared with their Maker. God walked with them in the cool of the day, a gentle presence that radiated love and peace, like the warm sunlight through the branches or the soft breeze upon the skin. Their hearts were open to listen, and the Creator's voice was like a lullaby of comfort and wisdom. This closeness made Adam and Eve radiant with innocence and trust; they lived in the light of God's care, shielded from fear, and wrapped in the gentle arms of His unwavering love. Their laughter rang through the garden like a sweet song, and their eyes reflected the bright hope that filled the earth.

In this tender beginning, we see how man and woman were not only created as beings of flesh and spirit but as neighbors to every living thing, teachers of kindness to all who shared in this world's wonder. Their uniqueness was a reflection of the Creator's heart, a heart that yearned not just for a beautiful earth, but for children who would cherish it, care for it, and grow in love beneath the vast skies God had spread out like a glorious tent. The garden was full of life, yet it was incomplete without the gentle footsteps of Adam and Eve, for in their hands lay the beginning of a story that would stretch far beyond the trees and rivers, a story about how love, goodness, and grace could grow in the hearts of those whom God had made in His own image.

And so we come to understand that in every child who reads these words, the same light shines, a spark of that original care and kindness, a seed of grace planted deep within, waiting to blossom. Just as Adam and Eve were given the sacred task of tending the first garden, so too are young hearts invited to cherish the world and to grow in the gentle ways of love, patience, and stewardship. For in every leaf, every creature, and every star that twinkles in the velvet night, there lies the echo of the goodness God wove into creation, and the tender promise that through kindness and faith, we all share in the beautiful work of making His world a place where grace may flourish forever.

Innocence and Joy

Playing in Eden

In the beginning, when the earth was fresh and new, and the sun smiled warmly upon the green fields, Adam and Eve walked in perfect harmony with all that God had made. The garden called Eden was a place of wonder beyond imagining, a tapestry of blooming blossoms and singing birds, where every leaf whispered the breath of life, and every breeze carried a melody of peace. Imagine with me, dear child, the soft grass beneath their feet, the gentle sun painting golden gleams upon their skins, and the quiet, tender voice of God walking with them, close as a friend, as they moved through this perfect paradise. There was no sorrow here, no shadow of fear or doubt, only a pure joy that danced like the fluttering wings of butterflies, delicate and free.

From the dawn, when the rosy light kissed the earth awake, Adam and Eve would stretch their arms upward and breathe the sweet air filled with the scent of blooming flowers and fresh, dew-kissed leaves. Their days were a symphony of laughter, light footsteps, and discovery. They were the very first children of the earth, and all the creatures looked upon them with curiosity and peace, for they walked in innocence, carrying the bright hope of a new beginning. They were friends too, not just with each other, but with every living thing, the lion resting beside the lamb, the birds nesting safely in the branches above, and the gentle rivers that sang over smooth stones.

Adam and Eve's play was a dance with the world itself; the garden was their playground, wide and endless. Imagine Eve gathering the ripest fruits from low-hanging branches, her fingers brushing the soft skin of apples and figs, her laughter bubbly as the fountain waters that shimmered nearby. Adam might call to her from across a glistening meadow, a sparkle of joy lighting his eyes as he showed her a bright butterfly, wings painted in the richest hues of blue and gold. Together, they chased the sunbeams as they dappled through the canopy, weaving between towering trees whose roots curled like ancient serpents beneath the earth.

Every corner of Eden told a story for their curious hearts to unfold. There were secret groves where the air smelled sweet with crushed blossoms, quiet pools where fish darted playfully beneath the water's glassy surface, and open fields where wildflowers bowed in gentle breezes. Adam and Eve would delight in these wonders, their voices soft and awed, sharing the marvels with each other as they learned the names of every bird, every flower, every creature God had lovingly placed in this cradle of life. Their friendship was a song of kindness and discovery, each moment a gift, each moment shining with the light of innocence.

At times, they would lie beneath the sprawling arms of ancient trees, gazing up through branches to see clouds drifting lazily across the bright dome of sky. Here, Eve might tell stories born in her heart, tales of what might come to be, of the love that stitched the world together like stars spread across the night. Adam would listen, his eyes reflecting the vastness above, feeling the tender truth of belonging to something greater than himself. Theirs was a world unbroken, where trust blossomed like wildflowers, free and fragrant, and the quiet promise of God's care wrapped around them like a gentle cloak.

In these moments, the pure harmony of Eden was a mirror to their souls, untainted and full of hope. They knew only kindness, only love, and the warm joy of friendship made whole. Every day was an adventure in gratitude, an unfolding story written by the hand of the Creator, whose voice whispered comfort and guidance. The garden sang with the beauty of creation, and Adam and Eve replied with voices soft and tender, joining the heavenly chorus in celebrating the gift of life.

Their footsteps were light upon the earth, as if the land itself cradled their passage, each step a blessing, each movement a hymn of grace. They gathered flowers to braid into crowns and chased playful squirrels through the underbrush, their laughter a melody blending with the songs of birds high in the branches. The animals, too, were part of this great dance; a deer would nuzzle Eve's shoulder, a curious rabbit would hop beside Adam, and even the great oxen would stand quietly, sharing the peace of this unharmed world. The bond they shared with all living things was pure and tender, a friendship born in the earliest morning of time.

When the sun climbed high, warming their skin with gentle heat, Adam and Eve would rest beside cool streams where the water danced over polished stones, clear as crystal and alive with tiny fish. Here, Eve might pick up a pebble, smooth and round, and hold it tight, marveling at the wonder hidden in such simple things. Adam, smiling, would tell her how God had fashioned every detail with care, from the lofty mountains to the soft moss beneath their feet. The world was a treasure chest opened wide, full of surprises and beauty, and in their hearts, a quiet awe blossomed, a reverence that nurtured their days and deepened their peace.

Their nights, too, held their own gentle magic. As darkness slipped softly over Eden, the stars would twinkle like diamonds scattered on a velvet cloth stretched across the sky. Adam and Eve would lie side by side on soft mats woven from fragrant grasses, watching the heavens unfold their quiet mystery. The moon, glowing tenderly, would send silver beams to caress their resting forms. In those moments, they felt wrapped in love, God's steadfast love that held them close, no matter what dawn might bring. It was the love that created all things, steady as the pulse of the earth, gentle as the hush of falling leaves.

In their innocence, Adam and Eve knew no fear, no shadow of sadness; their hearts were light, their spirits free. They spoke to God as a friend, sharing their thoughts and dreams in a language of trust and joy. God's voice was like a lullaby, soft and full of wisdom, guiding their steps and lighting their path. Sometimes, in the quiet of the garden, God would teach them of the stars and the moon, the animals and the sky, filling their minds with wonder and their souls with peace. In this sacred friendship, they flourished, their lives a testament to the gentle harmony of creation.

But more than anything, Adam and Eve cherished their friendship with each other, a bond woven from laughter, kindness, and shared discovery. When Eve found a nest of baby birds, she would hold them close, marveling at their delicate feathers, and Adam would smile, sensing the tender beauty of these small miracles. They spoke words soft as the breeze about the marvel of life and the promise of all things good. Their days passed like a gentle stream, clear and bright, carrying them through moments of gentle play and quiet reflection. In these hours, their hearts learned the preciousness of innocence, it was like a morning flower, delicate and bright, meant to bloom and grow in the light of love.

Their joy was a seed planted deep within their souls, a seed that would stay with them, no matter the path ahead. For in those times of pure innocence, they were close to God, close to the holy source of all goodness and light. Their eyes shone with the brightness of simple truth, and their hearts beat with a rhythm of grace, embracing the beauty of living in harmony with all creation. This was the gift of Eden, to know peace, to know love, and to know the great wonder of being held in God's gentle care.

As you imagine yourselves in this garden, dear reader, may you feel the soft touch of mercy and the bright glow of hope that shone upon Adam and Eve each day. May you, too, cherish the gift of innocence, that precious treasure of the heart, and carry it with you always as you grow and learn. Remember that just as Adam and Eve were loved in their play and friendship, you, too, are held close by a love that never fails. This love is a seed planted in your heart, ready to bloom with kindness, joy, and grace. So, as you walk through your own days, may you carry the gentle joy of Eden within you, a light shining softly before you, guiding your steps with peace and hope.

Walking with God

Before the dawn of sorrow and the shadow of sin, in a time when the earth was young and the skies pure, there was a garden so fair and full of wonder that it could only be called Eden. It was a place where the gentle hand of God had painted every blade of grass with shimmering dew, where the air was sweet like honey, and where rivers sang quiet songs as they meandered through the wide and tender land. It was here, amidst the blooming flowers, the towering trees, and the soft murmur of creation's breath, that God walked with the first children He had made: Adam and Eve. This walking with God was unlike any journey we know today; it was a sacred dance of friendship, a pure and unbroken fellowship between mankind and the Maker of all things.

In those early days, God did not stand afar or speak in voices that startled the heart. No, His presence was gentle and near, like the warm sun upon the skin or the soft whisper of a breeze through the leaves. Adam and Eve felt this closeness deep within their souls, a quiet joy that bubbled up in laughter and the lightness of their steps. They knew not the fear that troubles the heart now, for in Eden, the innocence of their hearts was a precious garment woven by the hand of God Himself. It shielded them from all shadows and led their spirits to dance in the open fields of peace and trust. Every morning, as the light spilled gold over the land, they rose with eager hearts, ready to explore the countless wonders laid before them by their benevolent Creator.

To walk with God then was to share in a relationship so intimate that the very earth seemed to sing in celebration of it. It was not a walk measured by distance or bent on reaching some far-off goal, but a steady, gentle companionship, as if the heavens themselves had bent low to hold their hands. When Adam and Eve walked beside God, they did not only see Him with eyes of flesh; they understood Him in their thoughts and their quiet yearnings. Their hearts whispered prayers that were carried like sweet incense to the throne of heaven, and in return, they received a love so profound it filled all the spaces within them. In this sacred fellowship, every sigh of the wind and every rustle of the forest spoke of God's attention and care. They learned the language of creation, discovering that the world was alive with holy meaning and purpose because God was there, watching tenderly over all.

In innocence, the first humans knew what it meant to be truly free. They roamed the gardens without fear of harm, their bodies untainted by weariness or sorrow. Their minds were clear and bright, unclouded by doubt or shame, for every shadow in their hearts was banished by the light that shone from the very presence of God. Freedom in their world was not merely the absence of chains or limits but a blessing given by God Himself, a freedom to be all that He intended them to be, to walk in harmony with the world and all living things. This freedom was a gift wrapped in trust, for God taught them how to live rightly, not as masters demanding obedience by force, but as a loving Father guiding His beloved children gently toward goodness and joy. Theirs was a life of abundant peace, where every day unfolded like a page in a marvelous story written with divine care.

The joy Adam and Eve knew was unlike any happiness that comes from toys, treats, or fleeting pleasures. It was the deep delight of belonging wholly and unconditionally to God, the warmth that springs from being loved without measure, and the lightness of heart that comes from walking in perfect truth. In their innocence, they could share openly, laugh without worry, and love without hesitation. There was no need to hide or fear because their hearts were naked before God, pure and transparent as the crystal streams that wound through Eden. This unburdened closeness gave them strength and courage, for they trusted that whatever the day might bring, they were held by a love that could never fail or falter. And so, their days were filled with gentle conversations, moments of wonder at the world around them, and quiet times of rest beneath the leafy canopies that God had set above them like a tender embrace.

How precious then was that first walking with God, for it was the very beginning of all that was good and holy in human life. It made Eden shine as a beacon of hope, a place where sin had not yet broken the harmony and where hearts beat in tune with the heavenly song. To walk with God was to live in seamless connection with the source of all life, to share in the eternal love that nothing could destroy. It was a gift beyond all measure, a holy dance where souls were twined with the Creator's own light. Adam and Eve, as the first of God's children, knew what it was to be cherished and to cherish in return, their lives a reflection of the sacred bond intended from the very beginning.

As children read this story and listen to the soft voice of the narrator, they can imagine the garden not only as a place of beauty but as a world overflowing with love and innocence. The picture is one of bright eyes looking up at the sky with wonder, feet touching soft grass that seems to sing beneath them, and hands reaching out to the hand of God in joyous friendship. There, in that untouched land, the troubles of the world had not yet come, and the hearts of the first humans beat with a pure music of peace and grace. It was a place where every moment was a blessing, every breath a gift, and every step walked with God was a step in love's eternal embrace.

This walking with God was not merely a story of the past but a tender seed planted in young hearts, showing them what friendship, trust, and innocence truly mean. It teaches children that before sin cast its shadow, the world was a place of perfect harmony where humans lived close to God, bathed in His light and love. It awakens in them a longing for that closeness, a hope that one day, through the grace of Jesus Christ, they too might walk once more in God's presence, free and unafraid. In this way, the story of walking with God gently nurtures a child's soul, whispering that innocence is precious, and the love of God is a treasure always worth seeking.

In the embrace of Eden, under the tender watch of their Creator, Adam and Eve did more than live; they flourished. Their minds were as open fields ready for the sowing of goodness, their lips spoke words that echoed the purity of dawn, and their spirits soared with the lightness of a world unspoiled. Each morning they rose with eyes bright as the stars just fading from the sky, ready to greet the day with a heart full of thankfulness. In the cool of the evening, they rested beneath the spreading branches of the trees, their souls at peace, their friendship with God as sure and steady as the earth beneath their feet. This was innocence, the precious state of being free from the burdens of sin, wrapped lovingly in the light of God's presence.

This closeness was not silent, for God shared His heart with Adam and Eve through gentle words and quiet ways. He spoke not as a distant ruler but as a loving Father, teaching them about the rivers and the animals, the flowers and the stars. He invited them to join in the joy of creation, to tend the garden with careful hands and thankful hearts. They learned that every creature bore a piece of God's glory, and every leaf shimmered with His kindness. As they walked with God every day, they became students of His wisdom, discovering the wonders hidden in the simplest things, the flight of a bird, the sparkle of a dewdrop, the soft murmur of a honeybee. In this way, their hearts grew with reverence and wonder, building a foundation of faith that would endure even the darkest days to come.

The beauty of walking with God in Eden was found also in its perfect peace. There was no conflict, no fear, no anger. The garden was a place where hearts were gentle and minds were clear. Adam and Eve knew that they were beloved children, wrapped in a love so complete and unfailing that no evil could take it away. This peace was the gift of innocence, a life lived in harmony with God's will, trustful and unafraid. It was a peace that did not come from the absence of problems, but from the sure knowledge that God was near and that all things were held together by His hand. In this peace, the first humans could roam freely, their spirits light and joyous, their laughter ringing like bells in a clear sky. Theirs was a world where goodness blossomed like the flowers and where grace was the air they breathed.

To walk with God was to live in a world where love was the most powerful force, so strong that it shaped the stars and painted the sunsets in glorious colors. Adam and Eve knew this love in every glance, every smile, every gentle touch shared between them. It was a love that held no judgment, no anger, only warmth and acceptance. This love was the heart of God's presence among them and the promise of all that was to come. For though their story would change and darken with the coming of sin, this love would never disappear. It was the root of hope that would sprout anew in the life of Jesus Christ, the Savior promised from the beginning. Through this love, innocence was not lost forever, but planted like a precious seed that would bloom again in grace and salvation.

Children who hear the tale of walking with God in Eden can feel that same joy and peace stirring within their own hearts. They learn that to be innocent is to trust and to love freely, to live simply and joyfully in the presence of God's care. They understand that God desires this closeness with every child, inviting them to walk side by side through their own gardens of life. And though the world may bring challenges, the footsteps of Adam and Eve remind them that a pure heart, tender friendship with God, and a spirit full of wonder remain the greatest treasures anyone can have. This story is a gentle invitation to young souls to begin their own journey, to seek God's presence in every day, and to cherish the precious gift of innocence as they grow in grace.

The wonder of walking with God before the fall is a story not only of what was but of what still is possible. It teaches that even in a world touched by sorrow, the door to God's presence stands open wide. It reminds children that God's love is steadfast and that His grace can bring healing where there is hurt. The garden of Eden, with its peace and perfection, holds a promise, a promise that one day, through faith and surrender, every heart can come to dwell in the light of God's love once more. This promise is the seed of hope planted gently in the soul of every child, a hope that blossoms into a life of kindness, faith, and unending joy.

Walking with God in Eden was the beginning of a beautiful story, a story of love that began in innocence and will never end. It was the gentle hand of a Father holding His children close, the quiet voice that tells us we are safe and beloved, and the sweet song of a world made perfect in His sight. For Adam and Eve, it was a sacred gift, a precious time of peace and delight where their hearts beat in tune with the Creator's own. And for every child who hears this story, it is an invitation to walk with God each day, to live in His love, and to cherish the gift of innocence that is the seed of grace.

The Gift of Trust

In the quiet garden where the light of morning gently kissed every leaf and flower, God placed His most cherished creation: man and woman, called Adam and Eve. This garden was no ordinary place, it was a paradise crafted by the loving hands of God, a home where everything was pure, and peace flowed like a gentle river. In this place of wonder and beauty, God gave Adam and Eve a very special gift, a treasure more valuable than gold or jewels. This gift was trust, a sacred trust that came with great love and great responsibility.

God did not fashion Adam and Eve as mere playthings or servants hidden away in the shadows of His glory. No, He made them as His companions, friends who could walk and talk with Him, sharing in the delight of His creation. God looked lovingly upon Adam and Eve and breathed into them a spirit alive with curiosity, goodness, and innocence. He granted them freedom in the vast garden, freedom to walk beneath towering trees and to speak with the animals, freedom to gather the fruit from every tree save one. This freedom was wrapped in trust, a divine kindness that asked only for their faithfulness and obedience, not as a burden, but as a way to love and honor their Creator.

The trust God placed in Adam and Eve was a sacred covenant between the Creator and His children. It meant God believed in their goodness and their ability to choose rightly. He knew their hearts were pure, unmarred by fear or doubt, open like the clear skies above the garden. This trust was a beautiful expression of God's love, showing that He did not want to rule over lifeless servants but rather to share life with willing hearts. By trusting them, God invited Adam and Eve to participate in the harmony of Eden, where every day was a gift and every choice held meaning.

Within this garden, obedience was not a harsh commandment or a cold demand; it was a dance of love between God and His children. The one rule given, to not eat of the tree of the knowledge of good and evil, was not meant to frighten or restrict Adam and Eve, but to protect them. It was a gentle boundary, like the walls of a safe garden play yard, keeping them from harm and inviting them to trust in God's wisdom. By obeying, Adam and Eve would show their love for God and their willingness to live in harmony with His perfect plan. This obedience was the key to preserving their innocence, the precious gift of a heart untainted by the shadow of sin.

In tender mornings bathed in golden light, Adam and Eve would walk with God beneath the branches heavy with fruit. Their feet pressed softly upon the earth, and every breath was filled with the fragrance of blooming flowers and fresh grass. There was no fear in their hearts, only the joy of being known and cherished by their Creator. God's voice was like music, warm and full of kindness, as He taught them about the world He had made. Adam and Eve delighted in His presence, feeling a closeness so deep it sparked a light within their souls, a light that shone brightly in their eyes and in their laughter.

This closeness to God was a pure and sacred bond, a friendship built on trust and love. God entrusted Adam and Eve not just to care for the garden, but also to care for each other and for the world around them. Their hearts were open and tender, free from envy, pride, or fear. They walked with firm yet gentle steps, knowing that their choices mattered, that the trust God had given them was a precious treasure to be nurtured. It was a trust spoken not with words, but with each act of kindness, each moment of care, and each heartfelt prayer whispered beneath the canopy of stars.

And yet, this gift of trust held something more, it was an invitation to grow and to learn. God did not wish Adam and Eve to remain as children forever, but to become mature in love and wisdom. This journey was to be walked together, hand in hand with their Creator, who would guide them with patience and grace. The trust God placed in them was as vast as the sky and as deep as the ocean, inviting them to explore the beauty of life while always turning their hearts toward Him. It was the trust that allowed freedom, yet called for responsibility; it was the trust that was the foundation of true obedience: a willing heart choosing love because it knew love well.

In these first days of the garden, the innocence of Adam and Eve was as delicate as the soft petals of a blooming rose. They had no need for fear or hiding, for their hearts were pure and their fellowship with God was unbroken. This innocence was a gift bright and shining, a treasure that reflected the goodness of God's own heart. It was a time when trust flowed freely between God and His children, creating a world filled with hope and promise, where every leaf, every bird's song, and every breeze whispered the sweetness of God's love.

God's trust in Adam and Eve was a grand testament to His faith in human goodness, a trust that said, "I love thee with a love that will never fail, and I believe in the purity of thine heart." It was a trust that invited them to choose goodness gladly, to obey not out of fear, but out of a joy that springs from knowing one is loved and valued beyond measure. This is a gift given to all children, to you and me, a sacred reminder that God's love is always present, calling us to live with open hearts and to trust in His steadfast presence, even when the world seems dark and uncertain.

The story of Adam and Eve in Eden is a beautiful tale not only of beginnings but of the preciousness of trust and the importance of obedience born of love. It teaches us that to be trusted by God is to be honored and that to obey with a willing heart is to walk in the light of His grace. The garden's peace, the freedom to choose, and the closeness to God were all parts of this marvelous gift, a gift that invites each child to understand that trust is the seed from which love grows, and obedience is the joyful path that leads closer to God's heart.

So, let your young heart hold fast to this truth: just as Adam and Eve were entrusted with the garden, so too are you entrusted with the beautiful world God has made. Every time you choose kindness, every time you listen and obey, you are caring for the precious trust God has placed in you. Know that you are loved beyond all measure, that your choices matter deeply, and that obedience born from love opens the door to endless joy and peace. To trust God is to know that you are never alone and that His love will always guide your steps, just as it guided those first children in the garden of purest grace.

The Whisper of Temptation

A Strange Visitor

In the quiet garden, where the trees bent low with heavy fruit and the air smelled sweet with blossoms, a shadow moved in a manner quite unlike the gentle creatures that roamed the earth. The serpent, slender and shimmering with scales that caught the golden light, slithered softly among the grass and flowers. It came with a stillness that felt both curious and clever, its eyes sparkling with a knowing glint. The serpent was unlike any other creature in Eden; it was not burdened with innocence nor did it share the pure joy that the birds and beasts displayed. Instead, it carried within itself a subtle cunning and a voice that could stir the winds of thought in the tender minds of those who heard it.

One bright morning, as the dew still clung to the soft petals and the light painted the leaves with a gentle glow, Eve wandered through the garden alone. Her heart was light, and her eyes drank in the marvels around her, the song of the sparrows, the rustle of the leaves, and the sparkle of the river that flowed quietly beneath the boughs. She moved with a grace that seemed to dance upon the earth, her curiosity endless and her spirit open to wonder. But on this day, a different voice was about to reach her ears, a voice that did not hum the sweet hymns of creation but whispered questions as delicate as a breeze yet as weighty as the night.

The serpent watched Eve from beneath a fig tree, coiled amongst the roots where dappled light played upon his gleaming form. His tongue flickered in and out, tasting the air filled with the scent of honey and blossoms. He saw the innocence in Eve's wide eyes, the gentle kindness in her smile, and he desired to speak. Not out of cruelty, but because he knew the power of words to shift the tender hearts of humankind. Slowly, he moved, his scales rustling softly as he approached, and spoke with a voice both smooth and oddly compelling.

"Why is it," said the serpent, "that thou shouldst limit thyself to that which is given? Hath God truly said, 'Ye shall not eat of every tree of the garden'?"

Eve paused, startled by the question that lilted through the air like a melody, though tinted with something strange and unsettling. She looked at the serpent and wondered, for the creature spoke with a curiosity she had not known before, a question that tickled the edges of her understanding and stirred a flicker of deeper thought inside her.

The serpent's voice was gentle and patient, weaving words like a soft net cast out to catch hidden desires. "Ye may eat of the fruit of many trees, but why is this one forbidden? It seemeth a wonder that such sweetness should be denied, when all the rest of the garden is so freely given. Doth the Lord not wish thee to grow in knowledge, as the sun awakens the flowers each morn?"

Eve looked down toward the tree, the Tree of Knowledge of Good and Evil, larger and taller than the others, with branches heavy with fruit glowing like the sunset. The command was clear in her heart as it was in the word of God given to Adam and Eve: they must not eat from that tree, for it was the boundary set by the Creator. It was a sacred law, a line drawn to guard their innocence and the harmony of the garden. Yet now, with the serpent's whisper coating the air, Eve's mind wandered to places unknown. Was there more to know than the simple joy of the garden? Could not knowledge be good? Could not curiosity be a gift from God as well?

The serpent leaned closer, his eyes gleaming with the glint of a secret revealed. "Ye shall not surely die," he whispered, bending the truth just so, weaving hope with a thread of doubt. "For God doth know that in the day ye eat thereof, then your eyes shall be opened, and ye shall be as gods, knowing good and evil."

The serpent's words clung to Eve's heart like dew upon the morning grass, fresh, cool, and enticing. The promise of wisdom, of seeing the world with eyes unclouded, called to something deep within her, something brave and yearning. The fear of the unknown mingled with the thrill of discovery, and for a moment, the garden seemed both a sanctuary and a mystery, a place of obedience and a place where choices must be made.

Eve's thoughts swirled like leaves caught upon a gentle wind. She thought of the garden in its radiant beauty, the laughter of Adam, and the songs of the stars as they shimmered silently in the night sky. She thought of God's kindness, His voice like a melody in the breeze. And yet, the serpent's words bore down on her like a question that refused to be silenced. Was it wrong to seek? Was it wrong to desire understanding? And if she reached out, would she be punished, or would she find something more?

The serpent's gaze held her, steady and unwavering, not harsh but inviting, as though he offered the key to a secret door, a chance to step beyond the world she knew. "Only thou canst make this choice," he murmured softly, "to remain as thou art, or to grow in wisdom and see the world with new eyes. Fear not the fruit; for in it lies the knowledge that maketh man strong."

Eve's hand lifted slowly, trembling as it reached toward the shimmering fruit. The skin was soft to her touch, warm with the sunlight that filtered through the leaves. The scent was sweet, alluring, filled with the promise of secrets wrapped in golden light. A moment hung between them, delicate and heavy all at once, where choice and consequence danced upon the edge of time.

This strange visitor, the serpent, had opened a door in Eve's heart that she had not known was there, a door to temptation, to challenge, to the brave but uncertain journey of choice that every soul must face. It was not a command to sin, but an invitation to understand that in life, we meet moments that test our hearts, that call us to listen to voices not always clear, to question, to choose, and to grow, even when the path seems shadowed and unknown.

Eve turned from the tree, her mind a whirl of thoughts, her spirit both touched by the serpent's words and pulled by the quiet law of love that beckoned her back. The serpent slithered away, leaving behind the garden's soft murmurs and the memory of a strange visitor who came not only with a question, but with a lesson for all who would listen, that temptation is not a monster hiding in the dark, but a trial of the heart, a moment to learn the boundless gift of choice and the strength found in waiting and wisdom.

With a breath as gentle as the dawn, Eve walked back towards Adam, carrying in her heart the seed of a great story, the story of humanity's first choice, the delicate dance between innocence and knowledge, between trust and doubt. And though the garden remained as bright and beautiful as ever, a new understanding began to grow within her, a bitter-sweet recognition that the world is made rich and wide by the choices we make, the lessons we learn, and the grace that waits to embrace us always, no matter where our hearts wander.

Thus, the serpent's visit was not just a moment of temptation; it was a tender, solemn reminder that every heart will face voices both soft and strong, that choices carve the path of our days, and that through grace and forgiveness, we find the way back to love and light, no matter how far we go. In the gentle hush of Eden's morning, a child's heart can hear this truth, that temptation meets us all, but with each step, we grow stronger in faith, wisdom, and the endless embrace of gentle grace.

The Forbidden Fruit

In the soft and shining light of the Garden, where every leaf seemed to whisper and every flower bowed in humble grace, God had placed a special tree in the midst of that beautiful paradise. It was called the Tree of the

Knowledge of Good and Evil, and beneath its boughs grew fruit unlike any other fruit in the garden. The fruit was neither bitter nor harmful by its nature, but it bore a sacred significance wrapped in a simple, clear command from God Himself. To eat of this fruit was the one rule given to the first children of the earth, Adam and Eve. Their Father, who made the heavens and the earth, had said unto them, "Of every tree of the garden thou mayest freely eat: but of the tree of the knowledge of good and evil, thou shalt not eat of it: for in the day that thou eatest there of thou shalt surely die." These words were spoken not in harshness, but with a gentle love that mirrored the tender care of a shepherd guiding his beloved flock. It was a rule meant to teach, protect, and prepare them for the fullness of wisdom yet to come.

The Garden was a place of abundance where every need was met and where peace flowed like a soft river beneath the green leaves. Every bird carried a song of praise, and every creature moved in harmony with the Creator's will. Within this perfect harmony, the command given about the forbidden fruit stood as a sacred boundary, a tender instruction to help Adam and Eve understand that true freedom did not mean doing whatever one wished but walking within the loving guidance of the Almighty, who desired only the best for them.

God's warning was clear and tender, yet it carried the weight of consequence. "Thou shalt surely die," He said, not in a spirit of punishment but as the great Truth of choice and consequence. Life and death, good and evil, joy and sorrow would come to be understood through this simple decree. It was as if God had planted a seed of understanding in the hearts of His children, a seed that would grow into wisdom when watered by obedience and watered again in forgiveness should they stumble.

Eve, dressed in the gentle morning light, often wandered beneath the shade of the trees, her heart a garden blooming with curiosity and wonder. She marveled at the birds and marveled at the trees, knowing and trusting the voice of God who walked with her in the cool of the day. Yet, within her, there stirred the gentle flutter of questions and thoughts, much like the soft rustling of leaves in a passing breeze. What was it about this forbidden fruit that made it so different from the others? Why was there a rule that seemed so singular, so weighty among the countless gifts bestowed upon them?

God's rule was not meant to keep them in darkness or fear but to invite them to grow in trust, to learn that the greatest freedom came not from doing as one pleased but from walking in harmony with the heart of God. Sometimes, when the sun cast its amber glow across the garden, Eve would pause in silent contemplation, her eyes drawn to the tree that stood apart, a quiet monument of choice and consequence. The fruit hung there like a jewel, beautiful and ripe, and though it tempted the eye, the command of God was a steady melody in her heart, a refrain of faith and obedience.

The story of the forbidden fruit unfolds not merely as a tale of restriction but as a tender lesson about the nature of temptation, the quiet calling that stirs within every heart faced with choice. Temptation is often a whisper, a gentle voice that makes the wrong take the guise of the right, that dresses up doubt in the colors of curiosity. For Adam and Eve, as for all children of God, the challenge was not in desire alone but in the question of whom to trust most, the Creator who fashioned the world with love, or the subtle voice that might promise more than it could ever deliver.

As the days passed gently, a stranger came into the garden's story, the crafty serpent, whose voice slithered with cunning and whose words wound like ivy around the tender branches of Eve's understanding. The serpent spoke in riddles and promises, twisting the simple truth of God's command into shadows and half-lights. "Yea, hath God said, Ye shall not eat of every tree of the garden?" it whispered with a voice as smooth as silk and as chill as a winter's night. The serpent planted doubt where there had been trust, making God's loving command seem like a burden meant to keep them from joy.

Eve listened, her heart fluttering like a bird uncertain in the winds of change. The serpent's words painted a picture of freedom not yet known, a hope that eating the fruit would make her wise as God, knowing good and evil in a way that promised power and light. To a young heart, the promise of seeing clearly beyond the simple world could look like an invitation to greatness. The fruit seemed more than just a piece of sweet food; it became a symbol of a choice, between trust and doubt, obedience and rebellion, innocence and the bittersweet knowledge of the world.

But the warning of God remained ever true beneath the whisperings of the serpent, a steady heartbeat calling back to love and faith. To eat of the fruit was to step beyond the safety of the garden's innocence and to carry with it the burdens and blessings of knowing right and wrong as they truly are. It was a choice that would echo throughout all generations, a moment in time where the seed of sin and the promise of grace first took root within human hearts.

In this tender and fearful choice lay the essence of the human experience, the struggle to choose rightly when faced with temptation, to hold fast to the words of love and truth even when shadows dance alluringly at the edge of vision. God's command was not a stone wall to imprison but a loving guidepost, standing tall in the garden to remind Adam and Eve, and all who come after them, that while the world is filled with wonders, the truest joy comes from living within the grace and wisdom of the Creator.

Yet, the presence of the forbidden fruit also bore a hopeful message, that even when choices are difficult and temptations strong, the children of God are not left without counsel or comfort. The warning, though stern, was spoken in the voice of one who loved perfectly, who beckoned gently back toward the path of life and light. It whispered that growth, learning, and even mistakes would come, but also forgiveness, mercy, and the enduring promise that love conquers even the deepest shadows.

For every child reading this story, the lesson softens fear and builds courage, for it shows that temptation is a part of every heart's journey, a test not of failure but of trust. The gentle rule in the garden teaches that there is a way to say "no" when the voices of doubt and desire rise within, that by listening to the Voice of Love and Truth, every child may find strength to choose what is right. And even when mistakes are made, the story holds in its embrace the promise of grace, a grace that heals, restores, and leads back into the arms of the loving Father.

So the story of the forbidden fruit is much more than a tale of caution, it is a tender chapter in the grand story of love, the first lesson in learning that the choices we make shape the paths we walk, that God's voice is a steady light in temptation's shadow, and that in this gentle guidance lies the beginning of hope, healing, and everlasting grace. It beckons young hearts to listen closely, to honor the sacred boundaries set by love, and to trust that, even when faced with the most difficult choices, the hand of God is always there to lead them safely home.

Choosing to Listen

In the quiet beauty of the Garden, where every leaf whispered the grace of God's creation and the air was filled with a melody of peace, there stood a tree unlike any other. It was the tree of the knowledge of good and evil, its branches stretching wide and heavy with fruit, tempting to the eye and stirring curiosity deep within the hearts of all who dwelt near. In this perfect world lived Eve, the first woman, whose spirit was innocent and filled with the bright light of obedience, walking each day with her beloved partner Adam in the cool of the garden, accompanied always by the gentle voice of God. Yet in this place of harmony lay the tender beginnings of choice, a sacred gift and a profound responsibility that would unfold the story of humanity.

One day, as the sun cast long shadows and the breeze carried the scent of flowers, Eve found herself walking alone beneath the towering trees, her heart open and trusting. It was then she encountered the Serpent, a creature craftier than all the wild things that roamed. Soft and smooth of voice, the Serpent spoke with a subtlety that twisted truth and danced around words, weaving a web of doubt and desire. "Yea, hath God said, Ye shall not eat of every tree of the garden?" the Serpent asked, planting the first seed of temptation in Eve's heart. His voice, silky and persuasive, invited her to question the boundaries set before her, to wonder why certain fruits were forbidden, and if perhaps the limits were more about keeping her away from knowledge than protection.

Eve's heart, pure yet new to such deceit, began to waver. The fruit hung like a jewel, its color deep and rich, seeming to promise hidden wisdom and power. She pondered on the Serpent's words, and in her mind lit a flicker of desire, to be wise as God, to know good and evil not from afar but from within. The garden had always been a place of delight and ease, but the fruit called to something deeper, something that stirred a longing she had not before understood. It was not merely hunger for food, but a hunger for understanding, for choice. And so, in that fragile moment of decision, Eve reached out and plucked the fruit from the bough.

As her fingers closed around the luscious burden, a gentle trembling passed through her; the innocence she once held slipped away with the bite she took. The taste was sweet yet strange, awakening a new awareness inside her. Suddenly, the garden seemed different, the shadows lengthened, the bright colors dimmed, and fear crept softly into her heart, like the first chill of a fading day. She heard the voice of God walking in the garden's coolness, calling out, "Where art thou?" And Eve, now knowing, was afraid and hid herself amongst the trees.

The choice she made, though small in gesture, carried the weight of profound consequence. For with the knowledge she sought came the knowledge of loss, the loss of innocence, the loss of untouched harmony with God's perfect creation. The serpent's temptation had revealed a deeper mystery: that humans, gifted with the power to choose, must also bear the burden of those choices. Eve's decision was the first step on a path that would lead her and all her children into the wide, sometimes weary world of right and wrong, of sin and forgiveness.

Yet this moment was not one of endless despair but of tender awakening. Though the choice to listen to the serpent led to sorrow, it also unveiled the profound need for grace and mercy. Eve and Adam, standing bare and ashamed, felt the weight of their disobedience but also the gentle voice of God, who clothed their nakedness with skins, showing kindness even in the shadow of judgment. This tender act whispered a truth that would echo through all generations, that though humans falter, though they face temptation and sometimes choose wrongly, God's love remains, ready to teach, to guide, and to forgive.

In the lives of children today, the story of Eve's choice reminds us gently that temptation visits everyone. It may come in whispers or in dazzling attractions, asking us to step beyond the path God has placed before us. But just as Eve learned, every choice carries a lesson. Sometimes we choose to listen to the wrong voices, and we find ourselves feeling lost or afraid, much like Eve did in the garden. But even then, there is hope. The story does not end with the fruit or the serpent's cunning; it continues through God's boundless mercy and the promise that no one is beyond the reach of grace.

This story is a soft mirror held up to the hearts of young readers, showing that the freedom to choose is a precious gift, and with it comes the responsibility to choose wisely. It teaches that mistakes are part of being human, but they do not have to define us. Each day offers new opportunities to listen not to the serpents that entice us away, but to the calm and loving voice of God, who calls us back to the garden of peace and righteousness. The story frames temptation not as a fearful enemy but as a challenge to be met with courage and a heart open to learning and growing.

Through Eve's experience, children are invited to understand that temptation can be real and powerful, yet it is only one part of the story. They learn that it is okay to ask questions, to feel unsure, and to seek help when facing choices that seem difficult. Above all, they are taught that they are never alone; the divine presence walks closely beside them, guiding their steps and offering forgiveness when they stray. In this way, the tale of choosing to listen becomes a tender lesson about the delicate balance of freedom and obedience, urging young hearts to grow wise in love and kindness.

As the garden's silence returned after that quiet moment of reckoning, so too does the invitation remain open for all who read this story, an invitation to ponder the choices they must make, to understand the consequences that flow from those choices, and to embrace the promise that through grace, every young soul can find light even in the shadow of error. The serpent's voice may woo and warn, but the voice of God is the voice of everlasting hope, whispering always, "Come unto me, and I will give you rest." And in this resting place, where forgiveness blooms and grace flows endlessly, children discover that the seeds of grace can grow even from the hardest soil of human imperfection.

Thus, the story of Eve stands as a gentle beacon, not to frighten, but to illuminate; not to condemn, but to comfort. It speaks to the tender truth that while every heart may face temptation, every heart can also find redemption. Choosing to listen wisely is a journey, often begun in the quiet moments of decision, wrapped in the loving arms of a God who sees, who knows, and who waits with open hands and a heart full of mercy. This sacred balance of choice, consequence, and grace is a vital seed planted in the young spirit, nurturing a lifetime of faith, hope, and the courage to walk ever onward in the light.

The Shadow of Sin

What is Sin?

What is sin? It is a question as old as time, whispered first in the cool and fragrant air of the Garden of Eden, and it still stirs gentle wonder in the hearts of children and grown-ups alike. To understand what sin is, imagine two paths before you. One path shines bright under the sun, filled with flowers and laughter, where the birds sing and the rivers hum sweet melodies. This path leads closer to God's heart, a place of peace, love, and joy. But just beside it lies another path that winds through shadows and thorny bushes, where the sky seems gray and heavy, and the gentle songs of the world grow quiet. This is the path of choosing wrong over right, the path that the Bible calls sin.

Sin is like a choice made within our hearts, a turning away from the good things God has shown us, the things that bring life and light. It is when we say no to what God desires for us and instead follow our own way, forgetting the kindness, love, and truth that He whispers to us gently each day. It is not merely a mistake or an accident; it is a willful choice to step away from the goodness God made for us, and in doing so, it brings sadness, not just to God, but to our own spirits too.

When we sin, it is as if a soft veil of gray mist falls over our hearts, clouding the bright light of God's presence. We may feel a heaviness within us, a little voice deep inside that tells us something is not right. This is because sin breaks the beautiful friendship God wants to share with us. Just as a child might feel lonely and sad when left out of a game, so too does our soul feel a kind of loneliness when we sin. It's a loneliness that comes from knowing in our heart that we have done something wrong, something that separates us from the warmth and peace that God gives.

But why does choosing wrong make us sad? It is because God's love is perfect and pure, like a gentle river that flows smoothly over stones. When we sin, it is like dropping a large stone into that river, causing ripples and splashes that disturb the calmness. Our sin disturbs the harmony God created in our hearts and in the world. It is not that God's love stops; rather, our sin makes it harder for us to see and feel His love clearly. It's as if the mist hides the sunshine just enough to make the day feel cold and a little frightening.

Children may sometimes feel this sadness as a heavy feeling in their stomach or a shadow over their smile. They might know it as the quiet regret after saying something harsh to a friend or breaking a special rule their parents asked them to follow. Sin appears in many forms, small or large, but all sin comes from the same place: a choice to turn away from God's perfect way. It might be telling a lie, hurting another person's feelings, or being selfish when sharing is needed. Even the thought of envy or anger, when allowed to grow, becomes sin, separating our hearts from the joy God wants for us.

Yet, there is good news that grows like a tender shoot from the firm soil of this difficult truth. Though sin brings sadness and separation, it is not the end of the story. God, whose love is deeper than the tallest mountain and wider than the widest ocean, does not want His children to be stuck in this shadow. Instead, He longs to clear the mist, as the sun breaks through clouds after a storm, and to bring every heart back into the sunlight of His grace.

The Bible tells us that God sent His Son, Jesus Christ, to bring forgiveness and healing for all our wrong choices. Jesus understands what it means to be hurt and tempted, and because of His deep love, He offers a way back to the bright path. This means that no matter how far a child might wander down the wrong road, God's arms are always open wide, ready to welcome them home. Sin might separate us for a time, but forgiveness is stronger still. It is a bridge built by God's love across the deepest chasms of sadness, leading us back to His friendship and peace.

When a child understands what sin is, they also learn an important lesson about forgiveness, not only from God but toward themselves and others. It can be scary to admit that one has chosen wrong, but in doing so, the heavy mist begins to lift. Saying sorry is the first step of returning to the path of light, a step God cherishes dearly. He waits patiently, ready to forgive and heal the heart, restoring the joy that sin tried to steal.

Through stories and gentle teachings, children come to see that making mistakes is part of the human journey, but sin is more than simply making a mistake. It is choosing to stray from God's love when He shows us the right way. Still, they do not need to fear or feel alone. Instead, they can find hope in knowing that God's grace is like a bright seed planted deep in their hearts, a seed that grows into forgiveness, kindness, and a closer walk with Him.

Sin may seem dark at times, but with God's light, that darkness cannot overcome. The night may feel long and lonely, but the morning always comes with the song of birds and the soft light that warms the earth. Sin is a choice, yes, but God's love is the bigger choice, the one that reaches down to lift us up, to guide our steps back to goodness, and to make our hearts bloom once again with grace. In this gentle hope, children can find comfort and courage, knowing they are never beyond the reach of God's loving mercy.

As a child learns to recognize the difference between right and wrong, they become part of a grand story that has been told since the beginning of time, a story of creation, fall, redemption, and love. Sin is part of the fall, but strong and tender as a tree growing in the midst of winter, God's salvation blossoms perfectly. The heart that understands sin is ready to receive the gift of salvation, and through that gift, to discover the joy of living in harmony with God's will, shining bright in a world sometimes shadowed by wrong choices.

So, what is sin? It is the choice of wrong over right, turning away from the goodness God gave us. But at the same time, sin opens the doorway to forgiveness, because God's great love is always waiting, always reaching for us, ready to welcome us back into His joyous light. And this is a message a child's heart can hold close forever, a precious seed of grace planted gently to grow and flourish in love.

Sadness and Separation

In the beginning, the world was a garden bright and fair, full of laughter and light, where every bird sang sweet songs, and every flower blossomed in the warm embrace of the sun. Within this paradise walked Adam and Eve, the first of God's children, made in His own image, blameless and pure of heart. They walked with God in the cool of the day, sharing joy and love without fear or sorrow. But as the quiet breezes whispered through the trees, something came into that perfect place that would forever change the way the story unfolded. It was sin, the act of turning away from God's perfect will, that brought sadness where there had once been only gladness, and caused a great gulf to grow between God and man.

Sin is much more than simply making a wrong choice; it is like a shadow creeping quietly over the bright meadow of our spirits. When Adam and Eve chose to listen to the crafty serpent instead of their Father in Heaven, they chose to disobey God's loving commands. This act was not just about a simple rule broken; it was the first time that the tender harmony between God and His children was broken. Imagine the sadness that touched the garden then, as if the birds themselves sang with a melancholy tune, and the flowers drooped as if their hearts were heavy. The beauty of the world seemed to lose some of its sparkle. And in the stillness of that moment, Adam and Eve felt something they had never known before, shame and sorrow, feelings that shimmered like dark clouds in the sky of their hearts.

Sin causes a kind of sadness that is deep and real, much like when a dear friend moves far away, or when a child loses a cherished toy. But unlike a lost toy, sin makes us feel separated not only from others but from the God who made us with infinite love. This sadness comes from the knowledge that we have chosen our own way instead of God's way, and it weighs heavily on our hearts because God's love shines so brightly; when we turn away, we feel the coldness of that distance keenly. Just as a gentle child might cry when feeling alone, so too does our soul weep when it knows it has hurt the One who loves us best. Yet even in this moment of sadness and separation, God's love does not waver or fade, though our sin creates a veil between our hearts and His embrace.

When we walk away from God's light, it is as if our steps are taken in shadows, and the warmth of His truth feels distant and dim. This distance can feel lonely, like being lost in a forest without a path home. Our hearts become heavy, burdened by guilt and regret, and we begin to understand that sin not only causes trouble for others but also hurts us, for we are made to live close to God, and when sin pulls us away, we lose the joy and peace that come from His presence. It is like a small child who reaches with trembling hands for a loving embrace but finds only emptiness. This feeling of separation is the sorrow that seeds itself deep within us, causing tears that no worldly comfort can fully soothe.

Yet, even when we stray and carry the weight of our mistakes, God's heart is full of mercy and endless grace. The beauty of this truth is that God is not angry for the sake of anger; rather, His sorrow is like that of a compassionate Father who yearns for His children to return home. When Adam and Eve hid themselves among the trees, it was not because God had ceased to love them, but because the sweet fellowship they once enjoyed was broken. However, God's love is like the dawn that follows the darkest night, unchanging, steadfast, and eager to bring light back into the shadows. Though sin may cause sadness and separation, God stands ready to forgive and to heal, reaching out with open arms to welcome us back to His side.

The sadness brought by sin is often tied to feelings of loneliness and fear, for when we do wrong, we sometimes feel afraid to show our true selves, worried that God might not love us anymore. But the King James Bible tells us in the Book of Psalms that "though I walk through the valley of the shadow of death, I will fear no evil: for thou art with me." This means that even in our darkest moments of feeling apart from God, He is still near, waiting to comfort and guide us back into His light. Our mistakes may cause a painful distance, but that distance is never too great for God's forgiving hand to reach. The sadness is real, but it is not the end of the story, it is but the shadow before the bright dawn of forgiveness.

When children are introduced to the concept of sin, it is important that they understand that it is not to be feared as a punishment but recognized as something that can make our hearts hurt and keep us away from the friendship with God that we were always meant to have. This is much like how a child might feel when they have disappointed someone they love, there is hurt on both sides, and a hope deep inside to make things right again. Sin brings sadness because it damages the bond of trust and love between us and God, but it also opens the door to the wonderful hope of forgiveness. The King James Bible reminds us that "if we confess our sins, he is faithful and just to forgive us our sins, and to cleanse us from all unrighteousness." This promise is like a gentle hand reaching into the darkness, ready to pull us back into the warmth of God's grace.

Throughout the stories and lessons shown to children, the idea of separation caused by sin can be tenderly explained as a cloud that drifts between a child and the sun, making the light seem far away but never fully gone. Children can imagine this cloud as feelings of sadness, regret, or confusion that come when they make choices that are not kind or that hurt others. Yet, the loving sun, the heart of God, still shines beyond all clouds, awaiting the moment when the cloud will part. The lesson is that even when sin causes hurt feelings or makes us feel distant from God, the pathway back is always open. God's forgiveness is a bridge built with loving kindness, spanning any divide created by sin.

It is also important to show children that everyone experiences this sadness and separation at times, for no one is perfect, and all have fallen short of God's glory. But just as the dawn follows the night, so does forgiveness follow confession. When a child feels the aching of separation from God, they can be encouraged to pray, to speak honestly and simply to God as a child would speak to their best friend. These prayers are like tiny seeds planted in the soil of the heart, seeds that grow into trust and love, rebuilding the friendship with God that sin once strained. There is no shame in feeling sad or distant, for even in those feelings, God's love is the gentle shepherd who seeks to bring the wandering lamb safely back to the fold.

The next step after recognizing the sadness that sin brings is the beautiful possibility of healing and restoration. Stories of kind and loving children who make mistakes but then seek forgiveness help young hearts to see that God's grace is bigger than all our faults. When little hearts understand that sin is a mistake that can be forgiven, and that God's love never ends, the sadness caused by separation begins to soften, replaced by hope and peace. This movement from brokenness to healing is one of the greatest blessings, where children learn that no matter how far they may wander, the arms of God are always open wide to welcome them home with songs of joy.

In telling the story of sadness and separation caused by sin, we also teach the importance of kindness, repentance, and making amends. When a child hurts another or disobeys, the hurt feelings that follow are like small drops of rain on a tender flower, emphasizing how sin affects not only our relationship with God but also with those around us. Understanding this helps children grow in empathy and the desire to seek forgiveness and to forgive others, mirroring the boundless compassion that God shows to all. Each act of repentance and each word of apology builds back the bridge between us and God, knitting the fabric of love ever stronger.

Throughout all this, the gentle cadence of the King James Bible's language weaves through the lessons, its poetic rhythm helping children to remember that the story of sin and salvation is an ancient and holy tale told across generations. The words carry a sacred weight, yet unfold in gentle melodies that comfort and inspire, framing the journey through sadness and separation not as a hopeless tale but a pilgrimage toward grace and redemption. Children listening to or reading these words come to feel the beauty of scripture as a safe harbor in times of sorrow and the joyous song of hope when forgiveness is received.

Ultimately, the sadness and separation caused by sin are tenderly portrayed not as an end but as a beginning, a call to turn towards God, to seek His face, and to open our hearts to His healing love. The sense of loss and distance we feel when we choose wrongly is a gentle teaching, inviting us to understand the depth of God's love and the sweetness of His forgiveness. Like a child who drops a beloved toy and feels the sting of loss, we feel the pain of sin, but the loving Father offers us a new gift, the gift of grace, to heal and restore our souls. And so the story moves forward, from sadness to hope, from separation to reunion, and from sin to salvation, a story told in the softest voice and the kindest words, leaving children comforted and certain of one truth: God's love never fails, and forgiveness is always near.

The First Sad Day

After the sun had dipped behind the tall trees and the golden light of the garden faded into shadow, Adam and Eve sat just beyond the still waters of the river, their faces quiet and their eyes heavy with a new and unfamiliar feeling. It was as if the happiness that had once filled their hearts like sunlight now slipped away, leaving a cloud of sadness hanging over them. The garden, so full of life and colors, seemed to shrink around them, as if it too were mourning. In that moment, Adam and Eve understood that something deep and important had changed. They felt a weight upon their souls, a strange ache that they could not see but could feel with every breath. Their choice to eat the fruit from the tree, despite God's clear command, had brought something they did not want but could not escape, sin.

The garden had been their perfect home, a place where every footstep echoed with peace and every breeze whispered joy. But now, in that quiet stillness, they felt the heavy hand of sadness pressing down. It was a loneliness unlike any before, because it was not just a quiet place with no others near; it was the knowledge that they had disobeyed the One who made them and loved them most. Their hearts, once open and free like the sky, felt closed and shadowed. It was as though a gentle barrier had formed between them and their Creator, and they did not know how to tear it down.

Eve's eyes brimmed with tears, soft and glistening like morning dew, and Adam reached out to hold her hand, finding comfort in solidarity. They remembered how the morning had blossomed with laughter in the garden, how God had walked with them in the cool of the day, speaking words of love and friendship. The sweetness of that company now seemed distant, a tender warmth that slipped through their fingers like sand. They felt ashamed, a new feeling that prickled their skin like the thorns growing near the trees they once admired. Shame told them that they had done wrong, and it scarred their spirits with doubt and sorrow. Their hearts whispered questions they did not want to ask: "Have we lost God's friendship forever? Will He still love us?"

Their bodies, so used to the ease of the garden's perfect balance, now felt different too. The bright green grass no longer seemed soft beneath their knees; the air, once fresh and pure, pressed thick and heavy upon their chests. The birds sang still, but their songs seemed far away, as if the harmony of creation had shifted just a little, and the joy was uneven. Adam's shoulders bowed under the weight of responsibility, knowing that he had led Eve to this place of separation. He wished he could turn back time, to hear God's voice of command once more and to share in His perfect peace. But the choice had been made, and there was no undoing what had come from it.

In this new sadness, Adam and Eve began to understand the meaning of sin, not only as a breaking of a rule but as a break in their own hearts and in the beautiful world around them. Sin was like a shadow creeping over a bright and shining day, dulling the colors and silencing the laughter. It was the moment when love grew quiet and fear and sadness took its place. The garden was still, but something deep inside them had changed, and they felt as though they were walking a path through a fog that surrounded all they had known.

Yet even in their sadness, there was a flicker of hope, small as a newborn star shining faintly in the night. They remembered the gentle words God had once spoken, words full of kindness and promises. Perhaps, despite their sorrow and the distance that now stretched between them and the Almighty, forgiveness was still possible. Perhaps the great God who had made the stars and the trees and the rivers could mend not only the world but their hearts too. This hope, fragile and tender, was like a seed planted deep within their souls, a seed that would one day grow and blossom into the sweet mercy of grace.

Though they hid themselves among the leaves and the branches, afraid to be seen because of the choices they had made, deep within them stirred the knowledge that God's love was greater than any mistake. Their footsteps were heavy as they walked through the garden, but their spirits whispered a simple truth, that forgiveness and love would come again, like the morning dawn that chases away the darkness. The first sad day was marked by a new kind of understanding for Adam and Eve: that every choice mattered, that every disobedience brought a cloud of sadness, but also that mercy waited patiently to shine upon them once more.

As the stars began to twinkle high above and the cool night wrapped around the garden, Adam and Eve clung to each other, their hearts aching yet filled with a quiet yearning. They knew that the journey before them would be long and difficult, for they must now live with the consequences of their choice. But they also knew this, God's promise was not forgotten. He had spoken of a Savior, a light that would come to chase away the sorrow and bring healing to all hearts that turned back to Him. Though the garden's laughter was hushed, and the peace was veiled in tears, the story of grace was only beginning, and they were part of that story too.

In the silence of that first sad day, the garden waited and the earth held its breath. From the depths of heartache, a new hope was born, a hope that would grow through the ages, reaching even to the children who would one day read these words and feel the tender hand of God's forgiveness resting softly upon their lives. Though the burden of sin had entered the world, so had the greater gift of love, and in that love was a promise that no heart was ever too lost to be found again. Adam and Eve, wrapped in the quiet shadows of their choice, carried with them the seeds of grace, planted deep within sorrow yet destined to bloom with the everlasting light of God's mercy.

God's Promise of Hope

God's Loving Words

In the quiet moments when a child first hears about wrong and right, about the soft edges of mistakes and the heavier shadows of sin, there comes a whisper, a promise from the heart of Heaven itself. It is a voice that does not scold or threaten, but rather embraces and assures, gently reminding every little soul that even when the winds of error blow hard, they cannot uproot the deep roots of love that God has planted in His children's hearts. The words of God are woven with such tenderness and power, like rays of golden sunlight breaking through a storm, telling us that we are not abandoned in the dark but cradled in a hope that will never fade. From the very beginning, before the trees of Eden stretched high or the rivers softly sang their endless songs, God spoke promises that outlast all human failings, words of mercy that glow with the warmest light, shining toward a future filled with healing and grace.

God's loving words are not just distant echoes from a faraway place; they are living breath that reaches out to every child who feels the stirrings of sadness or confusion when learning about sin and the troubles it can bring. These words come as a gentle melody in the quiet heart's ear, saying plainly yet profoundly, "I will not leave thee nor forsake thee." They carry the sweet assurance that no matter how many times a child might stumble or stray into the tangled forest of mistakes, God's arms are always open wide, ready to gather them close and whisper forgiveness. This promise is not just a hope but a firm foundation, an unshakable truth that sin will never have the last word. Because God's love is more powerful than any darkness, it breaks through the shadows with a light so bright that it will guide all children home to peace and joy.

In the grand story of creation and fall, God's promise sparkles like a star bursting through the night sky, certain and steadfast. When Adam and Eve faced the sorrow of choosing wrongly, the heavens did not remain silent or cold; instead, God proclaimed a future filled with rescue and restoration. He promised that from the very seed of this brokenness, a Redeemer would arise, a Savior who would mend what had been torn and heal every hurting heart. These words, far from complicated or too heavy, are spoken in the gentle rhythm of creation itself, inviting children to trust that God has a plan far greater than they can imagine. It is a plan written with the quill of love and sealed with the heart of mercy, designed so that every child who listens might know that there is a way back to wholeness and joy, wrapped in the gentle arms of grace.

To understand these loving words of God, one must imagine a Father watching over His children as they learn and grow, sometimes falling, sometimes afraid, yet always precious in His eyes. Even when the children do not know the hardest lessons or cannot grasp the depths of sin fully, God's tender promise breaks through their uncertainties. It tells them that He will send help, not a harsh judge, but a friend, a guide, a Savior who carries the light of hope and the gift of forgiveness. This Savior, Jesus Christ, is the heart of God's promise made flesh. He steps into the story of the world with hands ready to heal and a heart ready to forgive, showing children everywhere that God's loving words are true beyond all doubts and fears. Through Jesus' life and love, the deepest wounds caused by sin are gently touched and made new, so every child can see with eyes of faith that God's grace is more than enough to cover all things.

The promise of help and hope is not a distant tale but a present and living truth that colors every moment of a child's spiritual journey. It is the sparkle in a mother's eyes as she tells bedtime prayers, the quiet comfort of a family gathering to speak of God's faithfulness, and the soft joy that blooms when a child first whispers a prayer for forgiveness. Even the simplest hearts can understand that God's words are like seeds planted deep within their souls, growing courage and kindness where fear and shame once dwelled. These seeds of grace blossom in ways both seen and unseen, turning each small act of love and each tender step of faith into a bright flower of hope in the garden of life. The promise stretches from the grandeur of ancient scriptures to the warmth of today's gentle moments, assuring every child that God's love never fails and that salvation is not just a story from long ago but a promise for every new day.

Children might wonder, "How can God forgive so big a mistake? How can He love me after I do wrong?" Here, God's loving words answer with a quiet strength, teaching that love is not based on what we do but on who God is, unchanging, faithful, and full of grace. The promise to send help means that God does not leave them to carry the weight of their mistakes alone; instead, He shares it, taking it upon Himself through Jesus, so that every child might walk without fear into His loving presence. This is the heart of God's message, a message wrapped in kindness and woven with mercy, bringing peace to restless souls and lighting the path with forgiveness. It invites children to come as they are, with all their questions and all their hopes, and find rest in the arms of a Father who delights in their joy and longs to heal every sorrow.

The beauty of God's promise shines in how it reaches down even through the hardest days, offering a hand to hold when sadness or guilt feels too heavy to bear alone. The words spoken through the King James Bible, with their poetic grace and timeless rhythm, become like lullabies for the spirit, soothing fears and building faith. They teach children that even when the world feels confusing and mistakes bring tears, there is a promise higher than all that: God's unfailing love, a love that says, "Thy sins are forgiven thee." It is a love that kneels beside every troubled heart, whispers hope, and lifts each child toward the bright promise of salvation. This promise is not just a hope for the future but a living spring of comfort and strength, flowing daily to refresh and encourage all who open their hearts to receive it.

The promise that God will send help is also a promise that children are never truly alone. In every joyful laugh and every quiet tear, God is near, guiding, teaching, and loving without end. This truth softens the hardest lessons and turns the heaviest burdens into opportunities for growth and grace. God's words teach that even when sin tries to make a child feel far away, God's love is always reaching out to draw them near. It is a love that will not be denied, a hope that will not fade, and a future filled with the bright dawn of new beginnings. Every child can hold this promise close, knowing that no mistake is too great, no shadow too dark, and no heart too small for God's great love to reach.

As children listen to these words, sung softly in their hearts and echoed through the stories of scripture, they begin to understand that the promise of help and hope is meant to inspire courage, to awaken faith, and to nurture the gentle growth of grace within their lives. With every turning page, every prayer said, and every loving lesson learned, the seeds of this promise take root and flourish, transforming fear into trust, sadness into joy, and doubt into steadfast belief. God's loving words become a treasured gift, a lifelong companion, and a beacon of light guiding young hearts through all the days to come.

And so, children learn not only to hear God's promise but to live within its bright embrace, to walk with hopeful hearts, to love with overflowing kindness, and to share the grace that they have received. They are invited to trust in the Savior sent from heaven, to know that no sin is beyond forgiveness, and that each day holds a fresh chance to grow closer to God's endless mercy. Through these loving words, the journey of faith begins, tender and strong, leading every child toward a life bathed in light, held in love, and blossoming with the everlasting hope of salvation.

A Seed of Grace

In the vast garden of God's creation, where every leaf and every star shone with the beauty of His handiwork, there blossomed a special treasure known as grace. It is a word that dances softly on the tongue, whispering of kindness and love far greater than the brightest flower or the most wondrous sunset. Grace is the gentle gift bestowed from the heart of God, a love so deep and so tender that it reaches beyond the failings of humankind, wrapping around each child as the warm light of the morning sun embraces the earth. Imagine, dear little ones, that you are planting a tiny seed in your soul, a seed called grace. This seed is not like the ones you see in the garden that need water and sunlight to grow. No, this seed grows within you because God Himself places it there, watering it with His goodness and kindness, nourishing it with His unfailing love.

When we think about grace, we think about a gift freely given, not because we earned it, nor because we did all the good things or were perfect in every way, but simply because God loves us beyond measure. It is as if God reached down from the heavens, opened His hands wide, and poured out a shower of blessings upon the earth, inviting each one of us to receive them without fear or hesitation. This grace is a balm, a healing touch for the wounds that happen when we make mistakes or choose the wrong path. Sin, as we have learned, is like a shadow that tries to hide the light of goodness in our hearts, but grace shines even brighter, cutting through the darkness with the brilliance of forgiveness and hope.

Consider the story of a little child who fell and scraped a knee while playing in the garden. The pain was sharp, and tears welled up in the child's eyes. But then came a gentle hand, offering a soft cloth to clean the wound and a loving embrace that made the ache less frightening. Grace is much like that loving hand and gentle embrace, the comforting presence of God that consoles us when we stumble and fall. It reminds us that no matter what troubles come our way or how far we wander from the path of goodness, God's love is always ready to catch us, to lift us up, and to send us forth with renewed strength.

The Bible tells us in words rich and resplendent that grace is the very heart of God toward us. It is the promise that though we have sinned and sometimes feel unworthy, we are still chosen and cherished by Him. This promise shines through the tender teachings of Jesus Christ, the Savior who came to show us how great God's love truly is. Jesus, with His gentle voice and caring touch, brought forth the ultimate gift of grace, offering Himself so that all might be forgiven, healed, and made whole. Through Him, the seed of grace grows into a mighty tree, sheltering us in its wide branches, offering fruit of joy, peace, and kindness.

To understand grace more fully, let us imagine a vast ocean stretching farther than the eye can see, calm and deep, sparkling under the sun. No matter how many drops of water are taken away, the ocean remains full, never emptying. God's grace is like that ocean, endless and overflowing. When we feel small and unworthy, it is as though we reach out with empty hands hoping for a drop of mercy. Yet God's grace floods us with more than we can hold, filling the deepest parts of our being with His steadfast love. He does not ration it or hide it away, but pours it freely on all who come to Him with open hearts.

The beautiful truth about grace is not only that it covers us when we falter, but that it calls us to grow. When the seed of grace is planted in a child's heart, it begins a wondrous journey. It awakens a gentle strength, the desire to do good and to walk in kindness. It teaches that even when mistakes are made, there is always the chance to choose again, to say "I am sorry," to forgive, and to love anew. Grace is the tender whisper encouraging us to be patient, to be gentle with ourselves and with others, knowing that God's love patiently guides us all. It is the unseen hand that helps us stretch beyond our fears, to help a friend, to share a smile, or to show kindness when it is hardest.

In this way, grace becomes not only a gift received but a gift given. As we understand God's overflowing love and forgiveness, our hearts bloom with the desire to share that same grace with others. It is like a sacred dance where love flows from God into us, and from us to the world around. The Savior's words, spoken long ago but alive even now, remind us to forgive as we are forgiven, to love as we are loved, and to serve without counting the cost. Young hearts, as you walk through life, carry this seed of grace within you, nurturing it with prayers and gentle acts of kindness, and watch it grow into a bright light that warms everyone it touches.

Grace is the gentle truth that sin will not have the final word. It is the promise that no matter the shadows that may fall upon our path, there is a dawn awaiting with the morning's bright hope. It reassures us that God's plan for forgiveness and restoration is steadfast and sure. The King James Bible proclaims this hope in words that echo with beauty and power, saying, "But God commendeth his love toward us, in that, while we were yet sinners, Christ died for us." What a wondrous gift it is, that even when we did not deserve it, God's grace was poured out upon us, opening the way for salvation, joy, and eternal peace.

So, dear children, as you plant your own seed of grace, remember that it is the beginning of a lifelong garden. It is a gift that grows with every kind word, every prayer, and every loving deed. It is the hand of God holding you close, whispering that you are beloved, that you belong, and that nothing can separate you from His unfailing love. Let this seed take root in your heart, grow strong with trust in God's promises, and bloom into a life of faith, hope, and boundless grace. For in this seed lies the greatest treasure of all, the tender assurance that you are never alone, and that love, perfect and eternal, watches over you now and forevermore.

Waiting with Faith

In the quiet moments when the day slips into evening, and the stars begin their nightly dance across the velvet sky, there is a gentle stillness that invites us to wait. It is in this waiting that faith finds its true home. To wait with faith is not merely to sit and do nothing; rather, it is to hold a tender trust in our hearts, believing in promises not yet seen, clinging to hope that stretches beyond the present moment. Imagine, dear child, the garden before it blooms with colors bright and fragrance sweet. The seeds lie beneath the soil, resting in the dark, hidden from sight, yet within them stirs the life that one day will burst forth in glorious blossom. So too is our trust in God's plan, a seed planted in patience, nurtured by quiet hope, awaiting the perfect time to grow and reveal its beauty.

There are times in life when the shadow of sorrow or the weight of doubt feels heavy upon our shoulders. We may wonder why some prayers seem to linger unanswered, or why the hurt caused by sin and mistakes does not quickly fade away. It is in these moments that the heart learns to wait with faith, for God's ways are higher than our ways, and His timing is perfect even when it seems mysterious to us. The King James Bible tells us, "For I know the thoughts that I think toward you, saith the Lord, thoughts of peace, and not of evil, to give you an expected end" (Jeremiah 29:11). Though these words are old and sacred, they sing with a fresh melody to every child today: God has a beautiful plan, a hope for your life and the world around you, even when you cannot yet see it clearly.

Waiting with faith does not mean we sit silently in sadness, but rather, we hold a warm light of trust in our hearts and keep walking each day, step by step, toward the bright promise God gives. Even when sin has clouded the world and brought sadness, God's love is deeper still, reaching out with mercy like the arms of a gentle shepherd gathering lost lambs. The promise of a Savior, Jesus Christ, shines like a guiding star in the night, assuring us that sin will not win, that forgiveness is offered freely, and that restoration is near. This precious promise was spoken long ago by prophets and whispered in psalms, holding fast the hope of all God's children who wait in faith.

Think of a little seedling brave enough to push through the heavy earth, reaching for the sunlight. The seedling does not see the whole sky or know how tall it will grow, yet it stretches upward, trusting the warmth that calls it forth. Just so, we must reach out with our hearts, trusting the good Shepherd who watches over us day and night, who will never leave His children in darkness or despair. The journey of faith is like a beautiful story, a story written by God's loving hands, beginning with our small steps of belief and ever unfolding toward the great joy of His salvation. In this story, God invites us to be patient, to keep believing that His promises are true, even when the road seems long and the answers are hidden.

Jesus, the Son of God, came into the world to be that living promise. He is the light that shines brightly in the deepest night, the Good Shepherd who laid down His life to save the lost. When Jesus was with His disciples, He taught them to trust God's plan, to believe in the hope of what was to come. Though they could not always understand the path ahead, He reassured them with words filled with gentle power: "Let not your heart be troubled: ye believe in God, believe also in me" (John 14:1). His life, death, and resurrection proved that love is stronger than sin, that grace is greater than guilt. Through Jesus, the brokenness of the world is healed, and the gift of eternal life is given to all who wait with faith.

To wait with faith is a daily practice, a choice made over and over again in small moments of trust. It means when you feel afraid or sad, you remember God's promises and whisper a prayer for strength. It means when you see the world hurt by mistakes and meanness, you hold fast to the hope that kindness and forgiveness will bloom anew. It means looking with a child's eyes, open, curious, and trusting, toward the wonderful plans God has laid out for you and for everyone He loves. These plans are full of joy and peace, of healing and new beginnings, for God delights in showing mercy and welcoming His children home.

God's promises are like a river that never runs dry, flowing gently even when we cannot see the water. Sometimes, waiting feels hard because we want to see answers right now, to know how everything will turn out. Yet, faith reminds us that God is at work beneath the surface, weaving together a tapestry of mercy and love that will unfold in His perfect time. The King James Bible repeats these sacred truths time and again, inviting us to find comfort in its words and to carry them like a lantern through the night. "Wait on the Lord: be of good courage, and he shall strengthen thine heart: wait, I say, on the Lord" (Psalm 27:14). These words are a strong and tender hug for our hearts, urging us to hold fast in hope and bravery.

Waiting with faith is also a time for growing kindness and grace within ourselves. While we wait, we can choose to be patient with others, to forgive those who have hurt us, and to show love even when it is hard. Just as God's mercy is endless, so too can our hearts expand to share His grace with everyone we meet. This gentle growth is part of the spiritual garden planted in each child's soul, a garden tended by prayer, trust, and acts of goodness. When we believe that God's plan includes us, we become part of the beautiful story of redemption, helping to spread light and healing in a world that needs it so dearly.

Let us remember the story of Abraham, a man who waited many years with faith for the promise God had made to him. Though he could not see the future, he trusted God's word and was blessed beyond measure. Just as Abraham's faith was rewarded, so shall all who wait patiently for God's promises find joy and peace. The hope of salvation is not just a distant dream, it is a living reality, shining before us like the dawn, ready to brighten our hearts with love and truth. God's plan of forgiveness through Jesus Christ is certain, and it reaches out to every child who opens their heart to believe.

Dear child, when you find it hard to wait, when questions fill your mind and the path feels unsure, close your eyes and feel the gentle whisper of God's love around you. Remember that waiting with faith is a beautiful way to say, "I trust You, dear God, even though I cannot see all the answers now." Your trust is like a precious seed planted in the soil of God's gracious heart, and with His care, it will grow into a tree of hope, strong, steady, and full of life. In every moment, God is near, holding you close, guiding your steps, and preparing a future filled with joy, forgiveness, and endless grace.

So, let us wait together, hand in hand with God, resting in the sure promise that sin's power is broken, and salvation's light has dawned. The journey may be long, but it is filled with love and hope, and at the end awaits a joy beyond imagining, a joyful reunion with the Savior who loves us eternally. Waiting with faith is not empty or lonely; it is a sacred invitation to trust, to grow, and to bloom in the warmth of God's everlasting love.

Stories of Kindness and Forgiveness

The Good Samaritan

In a land of hills and dusty roads where the sun shone warmly and the olive trees swayed gently in the breeze, there lived a great teacher named Jesus who often spoke in stories to help people understand the most important things in life. One day, a man asked Jesus a question, "Who is my neighbor?" and Jesus answered not with a simple explanation but with a story that would ripple through time, teaching all who heard it about kindness, mercy, and love beyond bounds. Imagine a man walking alone on a path between the city of Jerusalem and a town called Jericho, a journey that many travelers took but that was also known to be a place where danger lurked in shadows. As he walked, happy and hopeful, suddenly he was attacked by robbers. They took his belongings, left him bruised and broken, and they vanished like whispers in the wind, leaving him alone and in great pain by the roadside.

As the man lay there, hurt and helpless, two different people came down the road. First came a priest, a man dressed in fine robes who served in the temple and knew the law well. Yet, upon seeing the injured man, the priest did not stop. He glanced quickly away, busy with his own path, fearing perhaps the troubles or impurity of touching a wounded person. Then another passed by, a Levite, who was also a servant of the temple, someone who knew the sacred words and the holy rites. But like the priest, he looked upon the man from afar and chose to keep walking, leaving the poor traveler to suffer in silence. It is easy to feel sadness for the man lying there, but the story does not end in loneliness or despair.

Next came a Samaritan, a traveler from a neighboring country whom many did not trust and often looked down upon. Yet, when this kind stranger saw the wounded man, his heart was stirred with compassion that blossomed like a gentle flower in the desert. The Samaritan did not hesitate. He knelt beside the hurt traveler and opened his bag, pulling out oil and wine to cleanse and soothe the wounds, like a soft balm for pain and fear. He then lifted the man onto his own donkey, carefully balancing him as they traveled slowly toward safety. The Samaritan took the man to an inn, a place where weary travelers could rest, and stayed through the night to care for him. When it was time to leave, he gave the innkeeper money, asking him to watch over the man and promising to return and pay any extra cost needed. This humble act of kindness went far beyond the simple rules and expectations of the law; it was a heart overflowing with grace and mercy.

Jesus looked at those who listened and asked quietly, "Which of these three, thinkest thou, was neighbour unto him that fell among the thieves?" All knew the answer, but it was a question meant to open eyes and soften hearts. The man who showed mercy, the Samaritan, was the one who truly lived the law of love. He became a shining example, teaching that our neighbor is not only those who look like us or live near us, but anyone who needs kindness, even strangers and those different from ourselves. This story paints a picture of grace in motion, grace that moves gently through the act of helping without asking for anything in return, grace that recognizes the face of God in everyone we meet, especially in those who are hurting and alone.

For children, the story of the Good Samaritan is a tender lesson wrapped in the warm robes of the King James Bible's rhythm and beauty. It teaches kindness to be a seed planted in young hearts, encouraging them to look around and see not just friends but all people as neighbors worth helping, forgiving, and loving. It tells them that sometimes the road is hard for others, and even when they are strangers, they still deserve mercy. Perhaps the littlest child knows what it means to share a favorite toy or to comfort a sad friend, and through this simple story, they begin to understand that these little acts can be like the oil and wine, healing and soothing the wounds of others. The Good Samaritan walks with children as a gentle presence, guiding their hands to help, their words to speak kindness, and their hearts to open wide.

In a world where many are busy with their own journeys and worries, this story reminds us to pause, to look closely, and to offer a hand where it is needed most. It whispers that love is not just a feeling but actions wrapped in grace and mercy, weaving invisible threads that bind us all together as brothers and sisters. It is a call to be brave, to stand for kindness when it might be easier to walk away, and to be courageous in showing love even where fear or difference tries to build walls. The Good Samaritan teaches children and adults alike that mercy is the language of the soul and that each act of kindness is a blessing sent back in ways we cannot always see.

As children learn this story, they find seeds of grace planted deep within their spirits, seeds that will grow tall and strong, blossoming into lives that reflect the light of God's love. The story's poetic cadence, echoing with the words of the King James Bible, gently cradles their young minds and hearts, helping them feel the sacredness of mercy and the power of forgiveness. It teaches them that every person has worth, regardless of where they come from or what they have done, and that through simple acts of kindness, they too can be vessels of God's grace here in this world.

The tender mercy of the Good Samaritan goes beyond time, reaching children today, just as it reached those long ago when Jesus spoke under the sunlit sky. In each helping hand, in every shared kindness, the story lives anew, inviting each child to step into the path of love and mercy, to be a neighbor who heals rather than hurts, who binds up wounds rather than leaving them broken. It is a gentle yet powerful reminder that grace is not only a gift given by God but also a gift that flows through us, a light to be carried softly and shared boldly with all who cross our path. Through this story, young hearts understand that by loving others, even strangers, they are walking close beside the footsteps of Jesus Himself, planting seeds of grace that will grow forever.

Joseph Forgives

In a land long ago, where sand met sky and stars danced like diamonds on the darkest nights, there lived a young man named Joseph. His heart was full of dreams, like soft seeds waiting to burst into beautiful flowers. Joseph's spirit shone bright, and though his brothers often looked upon him with envy and anger, Joseph held tightly to the warmth of love and hope within him. You see, Joseph was the son of a man named Jacob, and though his family was large, Joseph was different, he dreamed dreams that told of great things to come, dreams that whispered of a future where kindness and greatness would blossom from trouble and tears.

But not all saw him with gentle eyes. His brothers, stirred by jealousy, carried heavy hearts filled with bitterness. They could not understand Joseph's joy, and in their anger, they made a grievous choice. They took Joseph far away, selling him into a land where he was not known, where his tears were mingled with foreign dust and lonely nights. Yet, even in the harshness of slavery and the shadow of prison walls that later bound him, Joseph's heart did not harden. It only grew stronger, wrapped in a cloth of faith and trust in God's plan, a plan as vast and mysterious as the heavens above.

Years passed like flowing rivers, and Joseph's wise spirit caught the attention of those around him. Through God's grace, he rose to a place of great honor, a steward of a mighty kingdom, a guardian over the storehouses of grain in a time of great famine. It was then that the broken threads of his past began weaving themselves into a beautiful tapestry of mercy and forgiveness. The famine that reached his family's home sent his brothers into the land where Joseph now dwelt, seeking bread, unaware that the man before them was the brother they had wronged.

When the brothers bowed before Joseph, they did not recognize the face that looked upon them with eyes full of sorrow and kindness. Joseph could have turned them away with harsh words, could have let the shadows of the past darken his heart forever. But instead, he saw beyond their wrongs to the deep pain beneath, he saw the seed of grace waiting to bloom in forgiveness. "Fear not," Joseph spoke gently, his voice like a soft breeze, "for I am Joseph your brother. Be not grieved, nor angry with yourselves, because ye sold me hither: for God did send me before you to preserve life."

In those words, children, rests a mighty truth, a truth that teaches us about the heart's power to forgive. Joseph knew well the sorrow of being hurt, but he chose not to carry bitterness as a burden. He understood that even in the darkest moments, God's hand weaves a pattern of hope and mercy, turning wrongs into the seeds of grace. Joseph's forgiveness was a light shining through the gloom, teaching us that kindness can heal the deepest wounds, and love can mend what seems broken beyond repair.

Imagine, dear child, the courage it must have taken to love those who had caused pain, to open his arms in mercy rather than closing them in anger. Joseph's story is more than a tale of hurt and healing; it is a gentle lesson from the King's own words, reminding us to hold fast to grace. For forgiveness is not forgetting, but choosing to see with eyes wide open, to look beyond faults and failings, and to hold holy the hope that love can transform every heart it touches.

So when you feel wronged or see others stumble on mistakes, remember Joseph, who found strength not in revenge but in mercy. Let your heart be a garden where the seeds of forgiveness grow tall, where kindness blooms even after the hardest trials. For just as Joseph's forgiveness saved his family and led them back to peace, your grace can be a light in the world, a quiet power that changes hearts and brings joy where sorrow once dwelled.

And so, let this story linger in your thoughts, a gentle song of forgiveness sung from the pages of the oldest book, a song that invites you to plant your own seeds of grace, and watch with wonder how, in time, they blossom into a life filled with love, healing, and peace.

Jesus Loves the Children

In the gentle hills of Judea many years ago, the sun shone warmly upon a crowd that gathered around a man whose words carried the sweetness of honey and the strength of the mighty oak. This man was Jesus Christ, the Son of God, who walked among the people not as a king of grandeur, but as a friend full of tenderness and love. The children, small and bright-eyed, with hearts beating soft and curious, longed to come near Him, to touch His garments, to hear His voice that sounded like the comforting call of a shepherd. Yet, at first, the disciples, busy with their tasks and thoughts grown large with worldly concerns, gently turned the little ones away. They did not see the true treasure that these children carried in their laughter and innocent questions.

But Jesus, knowing the pure gold hidden in these young souls, called them back with open arms that welcomed all. "Suffer little children to come unto me," He spoke with a kindness so deep it seemed to ripple through the air like a soft breeze in springtime. "For of such is the kingdom of God." This invitation was not merely a gentle command but a promise that the kingdom, the place of divine love and everlasting peace, belonged in the hearts of the small and pure. The children ran to Him without fear, nestled in His embrace, and He laid His hands upon them, blessing them with a love that knew no bounds, a love as vast as the heavens and as steadfast as the mountains.

In those moments, Jesus revealed the heart of grace, accepting all, lifting the lowly, and cherishing the meek. The children, unaware of their own preciousness to the heavenly Father, felt the warmth of His mercy shining upon them like the morning sun breaking through the darkest night. This scene spoke undeniably of divine gentleness; the very Word made flesh showed that kindness is not reserved for the strong or wise alone but is a gift for every tender heart. As the Savior blessed these little ones, He gave a living lesson to all who would follow Him: that true greatness in God's sight is to be found in humility and love, in the simple openness of a child's soul.

The love Jesus bore for children was a mirror of the Father's love for all people, especially those whose spirits were fragile and tender. It showed that no one is too small or too insignificant to receive the tender care of God's mercy. When children approached Jesus, He did not turn them away for their lack of knowledge or their smallness in the eyes of the world, but embraced them with a fierce compassion that said, "You are precious, you are chosen, you belong." This story, passed down through time, whispers to every young reader that they, too, are beloved by the Lord; that God's heart beats in harmony with theirs even now, calling them to know the kindness and forgiveness offered freely to all.

Many times Jesus showed His kindness by healing the little ones who were sick, by touching their heads and making the blind to see, the lame to walk, and the mute to speak. His miracles were acts of mercy, but also messages, they declared that the broken and the weak are seen and cherished by God's eyes, that no sin or suffering is too great for the power of His love. This same grace extends to every child who reads these words today, reminding them that they are never alone and that Jesus walks beside them, gently guiding and protecting. With each tender touch and loving word from the Savior, the image of God's immeasurable kindness comes alive, teaching children that mercy is not just a story to hear but a light to carry in their own small hands, shining brightly in a world that often forgets to be gentle.

In the soft cadence of His voice, children heard tales not just of miracles but of forgiveness, the tender unburdening of the heart when one is shown mercy instead of judgment. Jesus taught that no mistake is beyond the reach of grace, and no heart too heavy to be healed. With stories like the prodigal son and the lost sheep shining faintly in the distance, His interaction with children underscored the truth that they, too, are invited into this great story of redemption. The Savior beckoned them inward, inviting them to embrace kindness and forgiveness not as burdens but as gifts that grow within them like seedlings reaching for the sun. And so, children learned through His example that to love one another is to echo the very nature of God, who is love everlasting.

Witnessing Jesus' love for children called His followers to mirror that same compassion. Parents, teachers, and all who care for young hearts were reminded gently to nurture the seeds of grace sown by the Savior. Forgiveness is not only to be spoken but to be lived; kindness is not only to be taught but to be felt deeply and shared freely. The children who once crowded around Jesus continue to inspire those who guide the next generations to walk in the footsteps of mercy. Through patience, discernment, and unwavering affection, caregivers imitate Christ's heart, creating spaces where children may flourish in faith and love. This nurturing circle spins endlessly, a sacred dance of grace made visible in the world through the actions of those who heed Jesus' call to welcome, bless, and care.

Even today, the story of Jesus' loving embrace reminds children everywhere that they are valued beyond measure. It gently whispers hope into their young souls, assuring them that no shadow of fear or doubt can dim the light of God's unwavering love. When a child reads, "Suffer little children to come unto me," it becomes a sacred invitation still ringing clear, a call to approach the throne of grace with boldness and trust. This tender beckoning assures every child that they are seen, loved, and cherished; that grace is not just a word but a living presence that walks alongside them each day. In their laughter, their questions, and their quiet moments of prayer, God's love is planted deeply, ready to bloom into a lifetime of faith.

Thus, the kindness of Jesus toward children transcends time and touches every heart willing to receive it. It invites children to know themselves as beloved creations, shaped by the hands of a God whose love is tender and vast. It encourages them to reflect that love in their own words and deeds, to forgive, to show mercy, to befriend the lonely, and to live gently in a world so often marked by haste and harshness. In embracing these lessons, children become carriers of light, small but mighty, planting seeds of grace wherever they wander. And so, from the gentle hills of ancient Judea to every corner of the earth, the love of Jesus for little ones continues to bloom, a fragrant testimony to the enduring power of kindness, forgiveness, and divine mercy.

Jesus, Our Savior

The Birth of Jesus

In the quiet town of Bethlehem, under a sky strewn with stars like diamonds spilled across a deep blue velvet, a most wondrous event took place that would change the world forever. In a lowly stable, where animals breathed warm and soft and the air was fragrant with hay and the gentle hush of night, a child was born. This child was not like any other. He was Jesus, the gift of God to all people, a light sent from Heaven to shine upon the dark corners of the earth. Mary, His mother, wrapped Him carefully in cloths, laying Him in a manger, a simple cradle made from rough wood and straw. Though His place of birth was humble and plain, His arrival was the fulfillment of a promise spoken many ages before, a promise of hope, love, and salvation.

This birth was no ordinary moment, for Jesus came to bring a new path to those who would follow Him. The story spread quietly at first, whispered among shepherds tending their flocks on the hillside. These humble men, accustomed to solitude and the gentle whispers of the night wind, were the first chosen to hear the glorious news. Suddenly, the heavens burst forth in brilliant light as angels appeared, their voices like music filling the air with joyful praise. "Glory to God in the highest, and on earth peace, goodwill toward men," they sang, their words weaving through the stars and into the hearts of all who heard. The shepherds hurried through the still night, their hearts pounding with wonder and awe, to kneel beside the newborn King. In that moment, they saw not just a baby, but the very presence of God's love made flesh, tender and true, a Savior come to bring forgiveness and grace.

Jesus' entrance into the world was gentle, filled with quiet love rather than grandeur or riches. He was born to live among us, to walk the earth as one of us, feeling the sunshine, the rain, the laughter, and the tears. His life was a gift, a bridge between the glory of Heaven and the struggles of human hearts. From that first breath, Jesus carried with Him the promise of salvation, a way to heal the brokenness caused by sin, a way to bring people back into harmony with their Creator. God sent Jesus to teach us how to love with an open heart, to forgive even when it is hard, and to show kindness to all, especially those who are lonely, hurt, or lost.

Throughout His days, Jesus spoke words of mercy and hope, stories that painted pictures of lilies in the field and birds in the air, reminding all who listened that they are cared for by a loving Father in Heaven. His gentle hands healed the sick, His arms embraced the sorrowful, and His smile softened even the hardest of hearts. But most of all, Jesus showed us the way to live by giving Himself for us, taking upon Himself the weight of all wrongs and pain, so that we might be free. This act of love, His sacrifice on the cross, was the greatest gift of all, a new beginning for every child who would choose to believe in Him.

To understand the birth of Jesus is to see the heart of God stretched wide open toward us. It teaches us that no matter how small or ordinary we may feel, each of us is precious in His sight. Jesus' humble beginnings remind us that God's love is not about grandeur or power, but about tenderness and compassion. Even in the poorest stable, with animals softly breathing nearby, the King of Kings was born. This truth comforts us, for it means God knows our needs and comes close to meet us where we are, with arms ready to hold and forgive.

The story of Jesus' birth is the beginning of hope, a seed planted in the soil of human hearts that can grow into faith and joy. When we whisper His name or sing songs of His coming, we join in a timeless celebration of good news for all people. Jesus is the Sun that rises to warm the coldest night, the gentle Shepherd who guides us through every valley. As children hear this sacred story, they are invited to receive the priceless gift of grace, understanding that they are loved beyond measure, and that through Jesus, they too can walk in light and kindness.

In this marvelous gift of Jesus' birth, we find the promise that darkness will not have the last word. Though stars may flicker and shadows may fall, the light born in Bethlehem shines forever, a beacon calling each young heart to know peace, forgiveness, and the tender embrace of a God who gave His only Son to bring salvation. This is the story that whispers in the quiet moments of prayer and echoes in the joyful songs of Christmas, a story as gentle as the newborn child cradled in that humble manger, a story of love that never ends.

Jesus' Teachings

In the gentle warmth of a sunlit day, among fields of blossoming flowers and the quiet murmur of children's laughter, there walked a man whose heart was full of love and kindness. His name was Jesus, and He came to the world not with swords or riches, but with a message as soft as a whisper and as strong as the mighty oak. Jesus taught the people many things, not with grand speeches or difficult words, but with stories and simple lessons that even the smallest child could understand. His words were like seeds planted in the hearts of listeners, destined to grow into trees of goodness and grace. Jesus showed that love was the greatest gift of all. He said, "Love one another, as I have loved you," teaching that love was not only for friends or family but for everyone, even those who seemed different or hard to love. He opened the eyes of the people to see that kindness was a language everyone could speak, through gentle words, helping hands, and patient hearts. His teachings invited children to imagine a world where each heart was a bright lamp, lighting the way for others by acts of compassion and forgiveness.

As Jesus moved among the people, He often spoke of the Father's boundless love, a love that was like the sun that shines on all, good and bad, rich and poor, strong and weak. He reminded them that no mistake was so great that it could not be forgiven, no wrong so deep that it could not be healed through God's grace. Jesus told stories that brought this truth alive: the story of the lost sheep who wandered far but was joyfully found, the forgiving father who welcomed his wayward son home with open arms, teaching that mercy was the heart's greatest treasure. These stories made children's eyes sparkle with hope, showing that God's forgiveness was a gentle hand reaching out, ready to lift any burden. Jesus invited everyone to come to Him with their troubles, to lay down their worries, and find peace. He told them, "Come unto me, all ye that labor and are heavy laden, and I will give you rest," offering comfort like a soft blanket on a cold night, reassuring young hearts that they were never alone.

With every step and every word, Jesus embodied kindness and the joy of serving others. He touched the sick, greeted the lonely, and blessed little children, saying they were precious in the eyes of God. His love was not distant or grandiose, but close and tender, felt deeply by all who met Him. He taught that greatness was not found in power or pride, but in humility and gentleness, "Whosoever shall humble himself as this little child, the same is greatest in the kingdom of heaven." Jesus drew children close, inviting them to see that their small acts of kindness mattered greatly in God's eyes. He showed that forgiveness was a gift and a way to live, telling His followers to forgive just as God forgave them, with full hearts and open hands. These lessons were like soft petals falling onto eager ears, planting a seed of understanding that grace is not earned but freely given, and that their hearts could hold this grace, making them lamps of light in the world.

Behind Jesus' gentle teachings was His great love, a love so wide that it embraced the whole world. He did not come to judge or condemn but to save and to heal. He showed by His own life that love sometimes asks for sacrifice, teaching forgiveness through His own willingness to suffer for others. Jesus willingly laid down His life as the greatest act of kindness, so that everyone might be free from the chains of sin and know peace with God. His sacrifice was like a bridge spanning a deep river, allowing no one to be separated from God's love because of the wrong they had done. Through His resurrection, Jesus proved that love conquers even death and that salvation was a gift for all who believed in Him. This gift of forgiveness did not come from human effort but from God's boundless mercy, which Jesus revealed in the most tender and powerful way possible.

Children who hear about Jesus discover that He is like a shepherd who watches over every little lamb, guiding and protecting them with a gentle hand. His words light a path through the darkness, showing that even in mistakes or difficult times, God's love remains steadfast and strong. His teachings encourage young hearts to grow kind and brave, to forgive and be forgiven, and to live each day as an expression of the grace He freely gives. Jesus' lessons are not just ancient words, but living truths that ripple through time, inviting every child to know that they belong to a family of love that never ends. Through stories and simple words, children come to understand that Jesus is their friend and Savior, who calls them to love and kindness, and who offers the greatest gift of all: forgiveness and eternal peace. In learning of His gentle care and steadfast promise, their hearts are planted with seeds of grace, destined to bloom into lives filled with hope, faith, and joy under the everlasting light of God's love.

Jesus' Love for Us

When the world was heavy with sadness and burdened by mistakes, there came a light shining bright from heaven, a light so full of love that even the darkest corners of the heart could be touched and warmed. This light was Jesus Christ, the Son of God, sent down with a gentle heart and a tender purpose. From the moment He walked upon the earth, His life sang a song of love that every child could hear and feel deep within their soul. Jesus did not come as a king with crowns of gold or armies armed with swords, but as a humble friend, a kind teacher, and a loving shepherd. His footsteps were soft upon the ground, yet they left a trail of hope that beckoned all who felt lost or weary to follow Him into the embrace of God's mercy.

Jesus' love was shown not through grand gestures alone but in quiet moments full of grace and compassion. He touched the sick and healed their pain, not with magic, but with the power of God's love shining through Him. He spoke gentle words that lifted the spirits of those who felt forgotten, and His eyes, filled with kindness, looked deeply into the hearts of children and grown-ups alike, as if to say, "You are precious, and you are never alone." In one small act, He shared food with those who were hungry, a simple meal that became a feast of hope. In another, He sat beside the lonely, giving them warmth that no fire could provide. This was the love Jesus carried, the love of God made visible and real in every gentle touch and heartfelt word.

Understanding Jesus' love means knowing that He came to bring us back to God when we had drifted far away. When people choose to do wrong, hurting themselves and others, it creates a wall between them and God's perfect goodness. But Jesus came to break down that wall with love so strong that no one could stand against it. He taught us how to live with kindness and forgiveness, showing us how to love our neighbors just as God loves us, without keeping score or holding grudges. Jesus told stories, called parables, to help us see what God's kingdom is like, a place where even the smallest good deed matters, where the lost are found, and where love always wins.

The path Jesus walked was not an easy one. He knew that to bring us back to God, He would have to face great trials and great pain. Yet, He walked it with courage and with God's strength in His heart. When people misunderstood Him, when they were unkind and even hurt Him, Jesus responded not with anger but with forgiveness. His greatest act of love was giving His own life, a gift so great that words cannot fully describe it. On a rugged cross outside the city, He took upon Himself the sadness and wrongs of the world, so that anyone who trusts in Him might be freed from the weight of sin and welcomed back into God's family. This sacrifice was not where love ended but where it overflowed, opening the door to a new life filled with grace and hope for all who believe.

Because Jesus rose from the dead, victory over sin and death has been won forever. This means that no matter what mistakes are made, how far one might stumble, Jesus' love is always ready to catch and forgive. His arms are open wide, inviting every child and every heart to come and find peace and joy within His care. To know Jesus is to know that you are loved beyond measure, and that love is not just for some, but for everyone, rich or poor, quiet or bold, young or old. It is a love that sees the good hidden deep inside, even when the world may not, and it gives strength to grow and bloom like flowers in the sunshine.

When children learn about Jesus, they learn about a friend who listens with patience, who teaches them to be gentle and kind, and who helps them understand that God's forgiveness is a beautiful gift, always available no matter the past. Jesus' life shows that love is more powerful than fear, anger, or sadness. It reminds little hearts that making mistakes does not mean God stops loving; instead, He offers a hand to help get up and start anew. Through Jesus, children can feel safe to ask for forgiveness, to forgive others, and to live each day filled with hope and joy. It's as though His love plants seeds deep in their hearts, seeds that will grow strong with faith, kindness, and grace.

In every story Jesus told, His words sparkled with truth and comfort, teaching children and grown-ups alike how to live lives that please God. He spoke of a shepherd who searched for a lost sheep, rejoicing more over finding it than over the ninety-and-nine that were safe. He spoke of a father who welcomed back his wayward son with open arms and a joyful heart, teaching that no one is ever too far to be loved and forgiven. Through these simple yet profound lessons, Jesus invites everyone to understand how important it is to love others just as God loves them, without condition, without limits, and with a heart full of grace.

Jesus also showed His love by praying to His Father in heaven, teaching children that they too can speak to God anytime, anywhere, with honest hearts. He taught the Lord's Prayer, a gentle way to talk to God, asking for daily help, forgiveness, and protection, and also reminding us to forgive those who wrong us, sharing God's love in our own lives. This prayer is like a warm hug from God, wrapping around each child who says it, assuring them that they belong to a great and loving family.

Knowing that Jesus carried our burdens and keeps us safe fills children with a sense of peace that can quiet even the fiercest storms within. His love is gentle but strong, patient yet earnest, and it never fades. It teaches that even when life feels frightening or confusing, Jesus is always near, guiding steps, healing hearts, and whispering comfort. His presence is like a calm river flowing softly through lives, bringing rest to tired souls and joy to happy ones, inviting children to trust and believe in the everlasting promises of God.

This love is not just for looking at but for living. Jesus invites each child to share His love by being kind, forgiving, and caring to everyone they meet. In doing so, children become little lights, reflecting God's love to the world around them, spreading warmth like the sun's gentle rays. Through acts of kindness, offering a smile to a friend, helping a sibling, sharing a toy, children echo Jesus' love and become part of the beautiful story of salvation, planted firmly in their own hearts and ready to grow.

Jesus' life teaches that everyone has value and that every act of love matters to God. No one is too small or too young to be part of His special family. He invites children to come close, to ask questions, and to grow in the knowledge of God's tender mercy. This inclusion is the heart of His mission: to gather all people, no matter where they come from or what they have done, into one big family held together by grace and truth. It is a family where love is the greatest commandment and forgiveness is the sweetest gift, given freely with joy.

As children hear these stories and absorb the gentle truths, they begin to understand not only who Jesus is, but who they are in God's eyes: beloved and precious, wrapped in love that never lets go. The story of Jesus is not just a tale to be told but a living hope that breathes new life into every heart willing to listen. It is a story that glows in the quiet moments before sleep, in the laughter shared with friends, and in the prayers whispered in the morning light. It invites young hearts to trust in a love that is strong enough to carry them through every challenge and gentle enough to hold them close like a mother's embrace.

Jesus' love for us is a fragrant flower blooming in the garden of God's grace, spreading its sweet scent far and wide. It beckons every child to come, to learn, and to grow, knowing that through His teachings and sacrifice, salvation is not just a distant hope but a living reality. His life is the greatest example of love and forgiveness ever given, a perfect reflection of God's heart. And in this love, every child finds a home where they are cherished forever, safe in the boundless arms of Jesus Christ.

Repentance and New Beginnings

Saying Sorry to God

There is a quiet moment deep inside each heart where the truth of our mistakes softly calls out, like a gentle whisper carried on the breeze. It is in these tender spaces that we find the courage to say sorry to God, not with fancy or complicated words, but with the simplest, most honest confession that we can make. Saying sorry to God is not about feeling ashamed or fearful; rather, it is about opening our hands and hearts to Him, giving Him the gift of truthfulness and the chance to heal the broken places inside. When we say sorry, we are turning toward God, beckoning Him to come close, to wrap His loving arms around us, and to remind us that His grace is greater than all our wrongs. It is the first step on a journey to a new kind of happiness, a joy that grows from knowing we are forgiven and loved no matter what. Imagine a child who has spilled water on their favorite drawing. At first, they may hide the wet paper, afraid of being scolded or thoughtless. But when they decide to bring the paper to their parent and softly say, "I'm sorry," something wonderful happens. The parent's face softens, their voice fills with kindness, and the child feels a warm glow of love instead of coldness or anger. This is much like saying sorry to God. God does not delight in our missteps or in our mistakes catching us unaware. Instead, He longs to meet us where we are, ready to listen, ready to forgive, ready to lead us back to the path of peace. The King James Bible tells us, "If we confess our sins, he is faithful and just to forgive us our sins, and to cleanse us from all unrighteousness." This means that when we tell God the truth about what we have done wrong, He promises to forgive us completely, wiping away the stain of mistakes as though they had never been. Think about how the morning sun chases away the darkness, flooding the world with light and warmth.

Saying sorry to God is like inviting that sunbeam into your heart, letting it melt away the shadows of regret and guilt, making room for light and hope to grow. In the quietness of prayer, children can find the words to speak to God as simply as a friend might talk to another, "God, I'm sorry I did that," or "Please forgive me for being unkind," or "I want to do better, please help me." These are not just words; they are the rising of a sincere heart, a heart ready to change and to receive new grace. Sometimes children worry that they must be perfect to be loved by God, but the truth is quite the contrary. God loves us even when we stumble and fall. Like a shepherd who searches for each lost sheep until it is found, God patiently waits for the moment we say sorry and turn back to Him. In a story told long ago, a father had two sons. The younger son took his share of the family's treasure and wandered far away, making choices that brought sadness and hardship. Yet, when his heart grew heavy and he remembered his father's love, he said, "I will arise and go to my father, and say unto him, Father, I have sinned against heaven, and before thee." When the son returned, his father did not scold or send him away. Instead, he ran to embrace him, rejoicing that his son had come home. This is a picture of how God welcomes us when we say sorry, no matter the distance we have wandered. Saying sorry to God is not just the end of feeling bad for something done; it is the beginning of a beautiful new friendship. It is the moment when our heart begins to mend, and the seeds of kindness, hope, and faith are planted deep within our souls. Every time we say sorry and ask for forgiveness, those seeds grow stronger, teaching us to be gentler with others and with ourselves. Sometimes, children may feel shy or unsure about saying sorry because they do not know the "right" words, but God does not require fancy prayers. He listens to the whisper of a small, humble heart willing to be honest. Imagine a garden where every apology is like a drop of rain nourishing the thirsty earth, helping flowers of goodness to bloom brighter and stronger. Through saying sorry, we invite God's grace to flood our being, washing away the dirt of mistakes, so that we can shine with a light that others can see and feel. The kindness shown by children when they say sorry to their friends or family is a reflection of the greater kindness God offers us. When children learn to say sorry sincerely, it is a gentle lesson in love, teaching them how to build bridges instead of walls, how to heal hurts instead of holding grudges. It is as if the heart learns a special song, sung softly in the quiet places of prayer, a melody of humility and hope that echoes throughout all creation. God's forgiveness is not only about wiping away what is wrong; it is about restoring us to the fullness of life that He intends for us. Like a mother who patches a torn dress with careful stitches, God works quietly in the background, mending our lives with threads of mercy and grace. When children say sorry, they are like little hands reaching out to receive that gentle mending, allowing God's love to make them whole again. And because God's love is so vast and never-ending, each time a child says sorry, it becomes easier to do so the next time, softening the heart and strengthening the spirit. It becomes a sacred habit, a joyful rhythm that brightens each day with fresh hope and peace. There is also a special kind of courage that grows when children learn to say sorry, not the kind of bravery shown in battles or great adventures, but a quiet, humble bravery that says, "I can admit when I am wrong and ask for help." This courage blossoms from trusting God, from believing that His love is stronger than all mistakes and failures. It is a courage that whispers, "No matter what, I am precious and beloved, and I can always come to God with my true heart." Sometimes, the things that feel hardest to apologize for are the ones that happen deep inside, a selfish thought, a hurt feeling, or a mistake made without others seeing. These hidden wrongs can weigh on the heart like heavy stones, but when children learn to bring those too before God, saying sorry honestly and fully, the burden lifts, and freedom begins. God knows every thought and every secret sorrow, and He waits patiently to heal all parts of us when we choose to turn to Him. The ways we say sorry can be as varied as the flowers in a field. Sometimes a quiet prayer is enough; other times, sharing a mistake with a trusted parent or friend helps us to understand and grow from it. What matters most is the genuine desire to make things right and the hope that springs from trusting God's grace to make us new. After the first honest confession comes the promise of a fresh start. It is like planting a tiny, fragile seed in the rich soil of God's mercy. With time, this seed grows, turning into actions full of kindness, words spoken gently, and life lived with a heart open to God's love. In this way, saying sorry becomes a powerful step towards becoming the person God has made each child to be, a shining light in the world, full of grace and hope. Throughout the day, children might find small moments to say sorry. Perhaps when they are quick to anger, or when they forget to share, or when they have been careless with their words. These moments, though small, are precious opportunities for God's forgiveness to flow into their hearts, washing away wrongs and making room for peace. As the sun sets low, painting the sky with colors of gold and pink, it is a gentle reminder that each day ends with an invitation to come before God and say sorry. Each night is like a quiet chapel, a special place where children can speak simply and honestly to God, knowing their words are treasured and their hearts are understood. And just as the stars sparkle brightly after the darkness of night, so too does God's forgiveness shine with a light that warms the heart and encourages rest. Saying sorry to God is not something to fear but a precious gift to embrace. It is like opening a door to a secret garden, where sorrow is transformed into joy, and mistakes are turned into lessons of love. It reminds children that no matter what has happened, God's arms are always ready to hold them, His ears are ready to hear, and His heart is ready to forgive. This loving exchange happens over and over again because God is faithful, He never grows tired of hearing our apologies or of giving us fresh starts. It is a beautiful dance of grace, a melody that sings through every child's life, offering peace that the world cannot take away. So whenever the heart feels heavy, whenever a wrong has been done, children can remember this gentle truth: God waits patiently, loving us perfectly, ready to receive our sorrow, to cleanse us from all unrighteousness, and to lead us into His everlasting light. Saying sorry to God is the beginning of a friendship that lasts forever, a friendship growing daily with kindness, faith, and the purest love.

God's Forgiveness

When we think about forgiveness, sometimes our hearts feel heavy because we remember the times we have done something we knew was wrong, or when we have hurt someone else, even if it was by accident. It is natural to feel sad in those moments, for our feelings tell us that we want to be better and to make things right again. Now, imagine a love so great and so tender that it reaches out to you no matter how far you might have strayed or how heavy your heart may feel. This is the love of God, who is always ready to forgive when we come to Him with a true and humble heart. The Bible tells us, "If we confess our sins, he is faithful and just to forgive us our sins, and to cleanse us from all unrighteousness" (1 John 1:9). What a beautiful promise this is! God is not angry forever; rather, He waits patiently for us to turn back to Him, holding out His arms to welcome us home with compassion and grace.

To understand God's forgiveness, we must first understand what it means to be truly sorry. It is not merely saying the words "I'm sorry" because we feel we should. True repentance is a deep feeling within our hearts, a sorrow for the actions or words that hurt others or ourselves. It is seeing our mistakes clearly and wishing to change, to grow into a better person, not out of fear or obligation, but out of love and desire to follow God's way. For children and all of us, this can sometimes be confusing because we might think that once we make a mistake, God will be angry forever and never want to be our Friend again. But God's forgiveness is different from anything else we know. It is not like forgetting because that would ignore what happened; instead, it is like healing a wound, making it clean and whole once more, so that the hurt no longer hurts us, and we can walk forward with joy and hope.

In the quiet whispers of our prayers, when we say to God, "I am sorry," with all the honesty in our hearts, we are opening a door to His wonderful mercy. Imagine a child who falls and scrapes their knee. At first, the hurt feels so sharp and sad, but when a loving parent gently cleans the wound and places a soft bandage, the child feels safe again, no longer afraid of the fall or the pain. God's forgiveness works much like this gentle healing, only much deeper because it mends the heart and spirit, where pain from wrong actions can linger. Each time we come to Him in honest sorrow, God's love washes over our hearts, smoothing away the sharp edges of guilt and filling us with a peace that can only come from knowing we are forgiven and truly loved.

The story of the prodigal son in the Bible shines brightly on this truth. There was a young man who left his father's house, choosing to live in a way that was not good for him. He made many mistakes and soon found himself lost and alone, wishing he could turn back time. The moment he decided to go home and say sorry to his father, something wonderful happened. Instead of anger, the father ran to meet him, embracing him warmly, celebrating not the mistakes but the return of his beloved son. This story reminds us that no matter how far we wander, God waits for us with open arms, ready to forgive and welcome us back into His family. Forgiveness is not about punishment or keeping score; it is about love that never gives up on us, love that sees our true value and our potential to be good and kind.

Sometimes, it can be hard to believe that we are truly forgiven. This is because our mistakes seem big, and our hearts feel heavy with shame. But God's forgiveness is so wide, so full of grace, that it covers every wrong, no matter how great or small. He promises that when we turn to Him, our sins, those mistakes and wrong choices, are as though they never happened. It is like writing with a pencil and then erasing every word so that the page is clean once again. The Bible says, "As far as the east is from the west, so far hath he removed our transgressions from us" (Psalm 103:12). This means that when God forgives, He does not just ignore our mistakes, He removes them completely from His memory because His love is so deep.

Forgiveness also brings joy, a joyful hope that we are not stuck or trapped by the things we have done wrong. Just as a flower can bloom anew after a cold winter, so can our hearts become fresh and bright when we accept God's forgiveness. It begins with a simple step: saying sorry to God, telling Him we want to be different and better each day. Then, God's grace lights the way, helping us to grow in kindness, in patience, and in love toward others and ourselves. We begin to see the fruits of forgiveness not only in our feelings but also in our actions, choosing to help rather than hurt, to share rather than take, to forgive others as we have been forgiven.

Many children find comfort in knowing that they do not have to be perfect to be loved by God. The truth is, we all make mistakes because we live in a world where wrong choices happen, but God's forgiveness teaches us that mistakes are not the end. Instead, they can be the beginning of a new adventure in growing closer to God and to others. Think of forgiveness like sunshine after a rainstorm. The rain waters the earth and helps flowers to grow, and so does forgiveness help our hearts to become stronger and more loving after we have been sorry for our wrongs. Even when we stumble, God's forgiveness gives us the courage to rise again and continue our journey of faith.

Sometimes, children wonder if they can ever be forgiven for something really bad they did or if they forgot to forgive someone else who hurt them. God's forgiveness is so powerful that it can reach anyone and heal any pain. It asks only that we come humbly, ready to say sorry and open to changing our hearts. As we learn to forgive others, we show that we understand God's love and mercy flowing through us. Forgiving others is one way to share the grace we receive, making the world around us a little brighter and more loving. When we forgive, kindness blooms in our hearts, and we become little vessels carrying God's light to everyone we meet.

The journey of forgiveness is not always easy; sometimes the heart feels heavy and the wrong choices seem too many to overcome. But each step we take toward God, filled with sincere sorrow and hope, is a step into His endless love. Even the smallest, simplest prayer of apology reaches the heavens, and God hears it eagerly, ready to wrap His forgiveness around us like a warm blanket on a cold night. He does not keep a list of our mistakes but keeps a heart full of love and mercy, waiting to help us start fresh.

God's forgiveness is an invitation to friendship. When we admit our errors and ask for His mercy, we are beginning a new story, a story of grace where mistakes no longer scare us but teach us and help us grow. God delights in our returning to Him, not because He wants to punish or judge, but because He longs to heal and bless us. This friendship grows each day as we learn more about His goodness and try to walk in His light, even when the path is difficult.

So, dear children, remember this: whenever you feel the weight of sadness from a mistake or a wrong choice, know that God's forgiveness is bigger, deeper, and kinder than you can imagine. Your sincere "I am sorry" is precious to Him, and with it, He covers your heart with mercy and love. Like a gardener tending to a special flower, God cares for you tenderly, watering your spirit with His grace, pulling away weeds of sorrow, and helping you to blossom into the kind, loving person He created you to be. Forgiveness is the first step toward joy, peace, and a close, happy friendship with God, who loves you always, no matter what.

Starting Anew

In the gentle unfolding of creation's tale, where every leaf and star sang the praise of their Maker, there came moments when hearts grew heavy and souls felt far from the light of God's presence. Yet the story of God's love is not one of endless sorrow or despair, but rather a beautiful journey of new beginnings, a chance for every child's heart to find fresh joy and hope in the kingdom of heaven. To begin anew is to understand that God always welcomes His children home, with arms wide open, ready to forgive and to heal. It is here, in the quiet whispers of the soul, where the most wonderful magic of repentance and renewal takes place, reminding us that turning away from wrong and coming back to God is like the breaking dawn after a long, dark night.

There is a whisper in the sacred pages of the Bible that calls to us, soft as a mother's lullaby, inviting children to know that no matter the mistakes made or the paths strayed, God's mercy flows endlessly like a river shining in the morning sun. When we read the story of the prodigal son, we are held gently in the arms of hopeful restoration. This young man, once distant and lost, choosing a path far from his father's house, made many errors along the way, but his heart filled with sorrow and longing led him back. He did not fear the messy clothes or tired feet that told of his wandering; instead, he spoke words that opened a door to grace, saying, "I have sinned against heaven, and before thee." And what followed was the most tender moment of all: the father, filled with compassion, ran to embrace him as though he had never lost him at all. This story paints for us, in the kind strokes of God's own hand, that repenting, saying sorry with all our heart and choosing to grow anew, is the sweetest step toward God's embracing love.

The journey of starting anew begins quietly in each soul, in a place so small yet so strong. When a child recognizes the shadow of wrong choices and whispers a humble "I'm sorry" to God, it is like planting a tiny seed of hope beneath the soil of their heart. The soil might seem hard and dry at times, but God's grace is like the gentle rain that nourishes that seed, and through His faithful care, it grows into a flower of peace, forgiveness, and joy. It is no sudden magic, but a gradual, wondrous unfolding, a renewal that invites the heart to bloom again, every single day. In the book of Psalms, David, a man who knew the deep ache of mistakes, prayed with a wounded spirit, saying, "Create in me a clean heart, O God; and renew a right spirit within me." His words are mirrors for children today, showing that even when we fall, God hears our cries and lovingly gives us a new start.

Like the story of Noah's ark, there is a powerful lesson about new beginnings hidden amid tall waves and pouring rain. When the flood embraced the earth like a dark blanket, it marked an end, but also a beginning. Noah, a faithful servant of God, listened to the call to prepare for a fresh start. The old world, with its troubles and wrongs, was washed away, and from the ark, new life emerged. The dove that returned with an olive leaf was a symbol of hope and restoration, whispering the promise that God's mercy is always beginning again. Children can watch this story and see that, no matter how big the storm, God's promise of new life and forgiven hearts sails steadily forward, carrying the seeds of grace for every soul ready to listen and grow.

Yet God's power to renew is not only found in grand stories or mighty floods; it also dwells in quiet, everyday moments. Think of Jonah, who once tried to run from God's call, only to find himself in the belly of a great fish, a place dark and tight, yet a place where God's grace waited patiently. Jonah's story teaches that even when we stray far or hide from what we know is right, God invites us to turn back with a heart full of repentance. And when we do, we come forth renewed, ready to follow the path God has lovingly laid before us. This reminds children that no mistake is too great for God's forgiveness, and every turning back toward Him is the start of something joyful and bright.

The beauty of starting anew is found not only in grand moments of Scripture but in the gentle transformation that happens inside every child's heart. When a little one feels the tug of kindness instead of anger, or chooses to share a toy instead of holding it tight, it is a blossoming of grace aligned with heaven's joy. Each choice to be better, to forgive, or to show love plants a seed that brings the soul fresh beauty. This growth is nurtured daily by God who delights greatly when His children walk in His ways, even if their steps are small and sometimes uncertain. Each day offers a radiant chance, a brand-new page, to write a story of love and good works that shimmer with God's blessing.

God's promise of renewal shines brightest in Jesus Christ, the Son whose birth was a gift of infinite mercy and grace to the world. Jesus came to show every child that grace is not just for grown saints but for all, large and small alike. Through Jesus' gentle teachings, healing hands, and ultimately His sacrifice, the pathway to being made new was opened wide. He said, "Verily, verily, I say unto you, If a man be born again, he cannot see the kingdom of God, except he be born of water and of the Spirit." This invitation to be born anew is a tender calling to all hearts to embrace forgiveness, to leave behind the weight of sin, and to walk forward in the light of God's endless love. For children, this means that no shadow is too dark, no past too heavy; rather, there is always a gleaming sunrise of hope awaiting all who seek God's grace.

The early disciples too were stories of transformation and fresh beginnings. Peter, who once denied Jesus, found in his heart the courage to repent and to become a rock upon which the Church was built. Children can imagine Peter's surprise and joy in feeling God's forgiveness wash over him, turning fear and failure into strength and faith. This power of God's mercy to turn tearful sorrows into joyful lives is a melody repeated through the ages, inviting every child to step into their own story of grace.

One of the sweetest examples of renewed hearts comes from the story of Zacchaeus, the little man who climbed a tree to see Jesus. When Jesus called him down and showed him kindness, Zacchaeus' heart overflowed with repentance and generosity. His story shows children that God's forgiveness changes not only feelings but also actions. When we say sorry, like Zacchaeus did, it leads to a life filled with goodness and sharing, making the world a brighter, gentler place.

In tender moments of reflection, children learn that starting anew is also about forgiving themselves. Sometimes hearts carry shadows of guilt or regret that feel too heavy to bear. Yet God's whisper is clear: "Thy sins be forgiven thee." When we accept His forgiveness, it brings true freedom, a lightness of spirit that lets us smile again and love again with full hearts. This healing of the soul is a gentle journey where God walks beside each child, offering peace as soft as a pillow and hope as certain as the stars.

Every day holds the promise of this graceful new beginning. Whether it is waking up with a heart ready to try kindness one more time, or saying a quiet prayer asking God to help when we feel weak, each act is a step toward the abundant life God longs for us to live. In these simple choices, children find joy in knowing they are always loved, always welcomed into God's family, no matter what yesterday held. It is a story repeated with each sunrise, a melody of mercy ringing through the heart's chambers.

So let every child know that no matter the mistakes, no matter the wrong turns taken, God's arms remain open wide, ready to gather them home. Starting anew is the gift of God's grace, the fresh bloom after winter's snow, the bright morning after a long night. It is an everlasting promise that each of us, young and old, may grow in love, kindness, and faith, with God lighting the path as bright as heaven's own joy. Through stories, through prayer, and through the gentle teaching of the King James Bible, 'Seeds of Grace' invites every child to embrace this beautiful truth: that the chance for a fresh start is always near, and through it, a happier, holier life with God awaits.

Living with Grace

Being Kind Every Day

In the gentle light of morning, when the sun's first rays stretch softly across the earth, there is a quiet invitation to be kind. Kindness, my dear children, is a seed that grows in the garden of the heart, blossoming each day when we choose to show love and thoughtfulness to those around us. It is not something grand or distant, but something very near and simple, waiting in the little moments of everyday life. When you smile at a friend who feels sad, when you share your toys with a brother or sister, when you speak softly to someone who is troubled, you are watering that seed of kindness, letting it take root and grow strong within your spirit.

Kindness is like the gentle rain that nurtures the flowers, not loud or boastful, but quiet and steady. Sometimes it may seem easier to think of only ourselves, to want what we desire without thinking of others. Yet, the King James Bible teaches us the beauty of love and grace, reminding us that the purest joy springs from giving, not from getting. A kind word, spoken with tenderness, can lift a heavy heart as surely as the morning sun chases away the darkness. Think of how powerful your voice can be when filled with kindness. A soft word to a friend who feels left out can make them feel seen and cherished. Even the smallest acts, like holding the door open or helping someone carry a heavy load, ripple outward in ways you cannot see but are mighty in their effect.

Remember the story of the Good Samaritan from the scriptures, who did not pass by the man who was hurt and left by the wayside but stopped to help with a loving heart. In just the same way, you can be a helper in your own world. When a sibling is upset or a classmate is lonely, your kindness is a bridge to their heart, mending hurts and building beautiful connections. It does not require grand gestures; the Lord looks upon the love within your heart, the willingness to give even when it might be easier to turn away. Even when you are tired, or when your own troubles seem heavy, kindness is a gift you can offer that costs nothing but means everything.

Some days, kindness asks you to be patient when another is slow to learn or makes a mistake. The patience you show, with a gentle smile and calm words, mirrors the endless patience God shows to us. Forgiveness, too, is a form of kindness, especially when someone has hurt your feelings or made you sad. Forgiving is not always easy, but it opens the door for healing and peace to enter your heart. Holding a grudge or nursing anger is like carrying a heavy stone; forgiveness releases that burden and lets your spirit soar free. In forgiving others, you plant a seed of grace that will bloom into joy and freedom, both in your heart and in your relationships.

Kindness also shines brightly in the way you care for your family. Your parents and guardians work hard to keep you safe and happy, and simple acts of love, a warm hug, a thank you, or sharing your smile, bring them great joy. Helping with chores without being asked or setting the table with care are ways to speak kindness without words. It is a quiet service, but God sees every little thing done in love, and it is a fragrant offering before Him, making your home a place of peace and light.

Friendship too is a garden that thrives on kindness. When you listen carefully to your friends' stories, offer your arm when they feel unsure, or invite a lonely child to play, you are planting flowers of love in their hearts. True friends are treasures, and kindness is the treasure map that leads us to them. Sometimes, friends may disagree or argue, but kindness is the grace that mends the fence and restores laughter. When you choose to say kind words rather than harsh ones, when you seek to understand rather than to blame, you become a peacemaker, a little ambassador for God's love among your peers.

Even in the bustling classroom, where many children gather to learn and grow, kindness can be your guiding star. When you share your crayons or your books, or when you help another understand a lesson, you are spreading warmth and light. Teachers smile upon such children who show the fruits of the Spirit, love, gentleness, patience, and God delights in these humble lights shining forth. Think also of those quieter moments when someone may be shy or new; a welcoming smile and a friendly greeting can be the beginning of a new friendship and a brightened day.

Sometimes, kindness involves courage, forgiveness is one such brave kindness, as is standing up gently for someone who is being treated unfairly. Even words of encouragement or a simple, "You are wonderful," spoken here and there, can give courage to a hurting heart. You hold within you the power to build others up, weaving a tapestry of goodwill and grace. This power is a reflection of the one true light, Jesus Christ, who calls us to love one another as He has loved us. To live in kindness is to walk as He walked, with a heart full of love and hands ready to serve.

And when the day draws to a close, and the stars twinkle in the vast heavens above, you can remember all the little moments where kindness was sown like seeds in the soft earth of your day. Perhaps you helped a friend, gave a compliment, chose helpful words, or forgave someone's mistake. Each act of kindness is a precious offering that pleases God, and it grows invisible roots in your soul, making you strong and beautiful inside. Never underestimate the power of a kind heart; it is the light that can shine brightly even in the darkest places, bringing hope and peace where it is most needed.

So, dear children, hold kindness close to you every day. Let it fill your thoughts and flow from your lips and hands. Show kindness to your family by listening and helping; to your friends by sharing and caring; to those who are lonely by welcoming and including them. Remember that kindness does not count how small or big; it delights in every little smile, every gentle touch, every forgiving word. It is a gift from God that you carry in your heart, a seed that will grow into a garden of grace, bringing joy to you and to all whose lives you touch.

In all these ways, as you go about your day, remember the tender words of scripture that teach us to be kind one to another, tenderhearted, forgiving one another even as God for Christ's sake hath forgiven us. Every kind deed is a step on the path of grace, a light shining in the world, a fragrant offering pleasing unto the Lord. So choose kindness, little ones, and watch how it transforms your day, your heart, and the hearts of all around you. For in being kind every day, you walk the blessed path of love, where God's mercy and joy abide, and you become a living seed of grace in His beautiful world.

Forgiving Others

In the quiet garden where the flowers stretch their colors towards the bright sky, there lies a gentle truth as wonderful as the morning light: to forgive is to open our hearts wide, just as God opens His arms to us when we ask for His mercy. Forgiving others is not always simple, for sometimes, the hurts that come to us feel like heavy stones that settle deep within our hearts, making us want to hold onto our sadness or anger as if it were a shield. Yet, the King James Bible teaches us in words both strong and tender that forgiveness is a gift greater than any treasure, a gift that we can give as freely as the dew falls each morning upon the grass.

Imagine a little child who has been hurt by a friend's unkind words or actions. At first, the child's feelings might swirl like a storm inside, strong and confusing. Yet if the child opens their heart to forgiveness, a calm begins to grow within, a lightness that lifts away the shadows and allows love and friendship to bloom once again. Forgiveness, then, is like a gentle rain washing away the dust, making the soul fresh and ready to grow.

The first step to forgiving others is to remember how much we ourselves need forgiveness. Just as every person has stumbled and made mistakes, so have we all needed God's grace to cover our flaws and bring us back to a place of peace. The Bible reminds us in Ephesians, "And be ye kind one to another, tenderhearted, forgiving one another, even as God for Christ's sake hath forgiven you." These words teach us that when God forgives us, He does so fully and joyfully, not holding our sins against us but instead welcoming us back into His love with open arms.

When we think of forgiveness in this light, it becomes clear that forgiving others is not something we do only for them; it is something that fills our own hearts with peace and joy, reflecting the endless kindness God shows us every day. Sometimes, forgiving feels like climbing a steep mountain, especially when the wrong done to us feels great or unfair. But it helps to remember that God did not just tell us to forgive, He showed us how through Jesus Christ.

When Jesus hung upon the cross, suffering pain and sorrow for our sins, He said, "Father, forgive them; for they know not what they do." This unimaginable love, offered even to those who hurt Him, reveals the very heart of God. It shows us that forgiveness is not about forgetting or pretending that wrong did not happen; it is about choosing to release the burden of anger and bitterness and instead holding onto love and compassion.

Forgiving others means we are brave enough to trust God's justice and mercy, knowing that He is the ultimate Judge who will care for every hurt and right every wrong in His perfect time. For a child learning this lesson, the story of Jesus' mercy can become a shining light in moments of difficulty, reminding them that forgiveness is a way to follow in Christ's footsteps and to live a life filled with peace and love.

In a small village, long ago, there lived two children named Sarah and David who were the best of friends. One day, David accidentally broke Sarah's cherished toy, a painted wooden bird that sang with the wind. Sarah's heart was heavy, for the toy had been a gift from her grandmother. She felt sadness and anger bubble up inside her, like a storm about to break. Yet, as she remembered the story her mother had read to her from the Bible about Jesus forgiving those who wronged Him, Sarah took a deep breath and decided to forgive David. She knew that holding onto her anger would only make her heart hard and lonely. The next day, she smiled at David and said, "It is all right, for I know you did not mean to hurt me." David's eyes filled with tears, and he apologized with all his heart. From that day forward, their friendship grew stronger, rooted in kindness and grace.

Sarah's choice to forgive brought not only peace to her own heart but also a chance for David to learn the power of mercy and to grow in love. This story, gentle and true, is like a seed planted in the soil of our souls, promising that forgiveness can heal wounds and build bridges where once there was only hurt.

Sometimes children ask, "But what if someone hurts me again after I forgive them?" This is a very wise question, for forgiveness does not mean that we must allow others to harm us or treat us unkindly. Forgiveness is about freeing our hearts so anger does not rule over us, but it also teaches us to choose goodness and to seek help when we need it. God's love gives us the courage to forgive while also being strong and wise. We can forgive and still choose to speak gently about our feelings, to set healthy boundaries, and to seek support from trusted adults or friends. Forgiving others, then, is not a sign of weakness but a brave and generous act of love, one that reflects God's own heart toward us.

Every time we choose forgiveness, we are like artists painting a beautiful masterpiece of grace and kindness. The colors of mercy and love blend together to brighten a world that can sometimes seem dark and broken. Forgiving others lights a path back to friendship and joy, helping us to see people with eyes full of hope and understanding rather than with suspicion or hurt.

When a child learns to forgive, they begin to blossom spiritually, growing into a person who chooses to live with compassion and peace. This beautiful growth is a testimony to the power of grace that begins inside the heart and stretches outward, touching the lives of everyone around us. The King James Bible, with its flowing, majestic words, reminds us in Colossians, "Put on therefore, as the elect of God, holy and beloved, bowels of mercies, kindness, humbleness of mind, meekness, longsuffering; Forbearing one another, and forgiving one another, if any man have a quarrel against any: even as Christ forgave you, so also do ye." These words invite us all, young and old, to wear forgiveness like a garment of light, shining God's love brilliantly in the world.

To help children embrace forgiveness in daily life, it is good to remember that every day brings small moments where grace can be practiced, a kind word spoken to a friend who may have been unkind, a smile given to someone feeling lonely, or the quiet choice inside a heart to release a hurt instead of holding onto it tightly. These tiny acts of forgiveness are like little seeds planted in the ground that, with time and care, will grow into mighty trees of love and peace. The heart that forgives is a heart that knows the sweetness of God's grace, and in forgiving others, we become more like Jesus, who showed us perfect love through His sacrifice.

One gentle way to understand forgiveness is to think of it as a thread weaving people together in a tapestry of kindness. When someone wrongs us, it may feel as if the thread breaks, leaving a gap. But when we forgive, we mend the fabric with golden thread, strong and beautiful. Forgiving is not always easy, for it asks us to be humble and to see beyond our own hurt to the goodness inside each person, just as God sees each of us with tender love, no matter what we have done. This act of mercy is a daily choice to live by God's light instead of shadows, to seek peace instead of strife, and to believe in the transforming power of grace.

Let us then remember the words of the Lord from the book of Matthew: "For if ye forgive men their trespasses, your heavenly Father will also forgive you." This promise is like a warm sun that shines on our spirits, assuring us that forgiveness is a joyful exchange, as we give it freely, so shall it be given to us, in love beyond measure. Children who learn to forgive carry this promise like a precious jewel in their hearts, a guiding star that helps them to navigate the twists and turns of life with courage and grace.

In the quiet moments before sleep, when the day's worries gently fade, children may speak a simple prayer like this: "Dear Lord, help me to forgive others as You have forgiven me. Teach me to love with a kind heart, to let go of anger, and to shine with Your grace. Thank You for loving me always." These tender prayers open the door to a heart transformed by forgiveness, making way for peace to dwell within and radiate outward. Forgiving others becomes not just a lesson learned, but a way of life, a path walked hand in hand with God's everlasting love.

So, dear child, when you feel hurt or wronged, remember the gentle words and stories that teach you about forgiveness. Know that it is okay to feel pain, but it is also wonderful to open your heart and choose to forgive, just as God forgives you. In doing so, you plant seeds of grace that will grow and flourish, filling your life and the lives of those around you with the sweet fruits of kindness, peace, and endless love. Forgiving others is perhaps one of the greatest gifts you can give yourself and the world, a gift wrapped in the tender embrace of God's mercy, shining bright forevermore.

Growing in Grace

In the dawning light of each morning, when the birds begin their gentle song and the world is washed fresh with dew, a tiny seed begins its quiet journey deep beneath the earth. Wrapped in the soft embrace of the soil, the seed listens closely to the whisperings of the sun and the kindly touch of the rain. In much the same way, a heart that is eager and open can grow in grace, unfolding little by little with kindness, forgiveness, and faith. Just as the seed does not sprout in haste but follows a steady, patient rhythm, so too does the soul learn to stretch closer toward the light of

God's love, growing stronger day by day. It is here, in the tender moments of learning and living, that grace takes root and begins to flourish in the garden of our spirits.

Imagine a small child named Eli, who lives in a cozy village nestled among green hills and sparkling streams. Eli's mother often tells him stories of the King's garden, where every flower blooms not because it is hurried, but because it is gently cared for. "Grace," she says, "is like watering that garden inside you. It helps you grow kind thoughts, soft words, and loving deeds." One morning, Eli finds his friend Miriam crying because her toy is broken. Though Eli feels a little sad himself, he remembers the story of the garden and chooses to give Miriam a gentle smile and his own small wooden horse to cheer her. This simple act of sharing is like a drop of rain on Miriam's sorrowful heart, helping it bloom anew. Through such everyday moments, children learn that grace is not a grand thunder, but a quiet, steady rain that nourishes the spirit.

The path of growing in grace also asks us to forgive, one of the most tender and beautiful seeds we can plant within our hearts. Forgiveness is a mighty strength cloaked in gentleness; it is the balm that soothes the wounds caused by misunderstanding or hurt. When a child is wronged by another, it can be as if a cold shadow falls over their joy. But if they can find it in their hearts to forgive, the shadow lifts, replaced by a warm light that heals and renews. Picture a boy named Caleb who feels angry because his friend took his favorite book without asking. Caleb's first thoughts are of upset and bitterness, but then he recalls the words of Jesus, who taught us to love and forgive even those who hurt us. With great courage, Caleb chooses to say, "I forgive you," and in that moment, he feels lighter and freer, like a bird released from its cage. This gift of forgiveness, given and received, is a blossom of grace growing strong within the soul.

Grace also grows when children make good choices, even when it is hard to do so. Life often offers moments of temptation and challenge, much like the serpents that whispered to the first man and woman in the

Garden of Eden. But just as Adam and Eve learned the weight of their choices, children too discover that their decisions shape the garden of their hearts. In the story of little Anna, we see this tender lesson come alive. One day, Anna finds a lost kitten, cold and shivering. Though it would be easier to leave the kitten alone, Anna decides to nurture it with warmth and food. Some of her friends tease her for caring so much for a stray, but Anna's heart is steadfast. She knows that love and kindness, even when unnoticed or unappreciated, are treasures in God's eyes. As the kitten grows healthy and playful, so does Anna's heart swell with joy, reminding her that each good choice is another sprout of grace rising toward the sun.

The nurturing of grace is also woven through the gentle art of praying and reflecting with God. When children bow their heads and speak softly with the Lord, they open a secret garden gate, inviting a tender light to shine within. Prayer is like a quiet stream that flows to refresh the soul, carrying away worries and filling young hearts with hope and peace. Little Samuel, who lives by the sea, often prays while watching the waves kiss the shore, asking God to help him be kind and brave. With every whispered prayer, Samuel feels a growing warmth inside, a steady hand guiding his footsteps. Prayer strengthens faith by reminding children that they are never alone, that the Lord walks beside them, offering grace as boundless as the ocean's deep.

Grace speaks also in the language of patience and understanding. It waits gently when things are not perfect or quick, teaching children that just as the seasons shift with quiet beauty, their hearts too grow in time. There is a soft magic in waiting, in trusting that fruits will ripen and flowers will bloom because God's timing is kind and true. In the story of Esther, a young girl learns to be patient as she waits for the right moment to show courage and love, teaching readers that grace is both gentle and strong, moving with the rhythm of God's perfect plan. Such lessons encourage children to hold onto hope, to carry kindness even when their hearts feel weary, knowing that grace is working quietly, unseen, within them.

Every day brings new chances to plant seeds of grace, through a smile to a lonely friend, a helping hand to someone in need, or a whispered "thank you" for God's blessings. These small acts, though seemingly simple, are the building blocks of a life filled with goodness and light. The stories of David's courage, Ruth's loyalty, and Jesus' tender mercy all call upon children to embody grace in their daily lives, to grow spiritually by loving God and each other with pure hearts. As they read and hear these stories, young hearts begin to understand that grace is not only a gift to receive but a treasure to share, a light to carry in dark corners and a soft cloak of warmth around those who need it most.

It is important to remember that growing in grace is not about being perfect, but about growing gently through our successes and mistakes alike. Just as a garden may face storms or droughts, so too will children face challenges and sometimes falter. Yet God's grace is the tender hand that lifts them, the promise that no matter how many times they stumble, they can always rise again. The story of Peter, who denied Jesus yet was lovingly restored, teaches that grace is a powerful renewal, inviting children to embrace their own journey with hope and courage, knowing that forgiveness and love are always within reach.

As children learn to live in grace, their hearts begin to blossom with the fruits of the Spirit, love, joy, peace, patience, kindness, goodness, faithfulness, gentleness, and self-control. These qualities are the blossoms in God's garden, showing that the seeds of grace have taken root and are growing strong. Through daily kindness and faithful living, children become shining examples of God's love, carrying the light of the scriptures into their homes, schools, and play. The gentle rhythm of these virtues guides them like a soft melody, comforting and encouraging, as they travel onward in their spiritual adventures.

To help these tender seeds grow, families and caregivers play a sacred role in nurturing faith and grace within children. Through shared stories, prayers at bedtime, and moments of quiet reflection, they plant and water the garden of the child's soul. Encouraging children to speak openly about their feelings and questions creates a safe space where grace can flourish without fear or judgment. When children see adults modeling forgiveness and kindness, they learn to mirror those virtues in their own lives. The warmth of family and community becomes like the sun, nurturing young spirits as they grow steadfast in faith.

In the gentle words of the Psalmist, "Like as the heart panteth after the water brooks, so panteth my soul after thee, O God." This longing for God and His grace is planted within every child, a quiet yearning to know and love Him more. As children embrace grace, they find that their hearts indeed thirst for goodness and truth, growing stronger with every step closer to God's light. Their faith becomes a tender garden, blossoming with promise, hope, and joy, ready to shine forth and bless the world around them.

Thus, the journey of growing in grace is a beautiful unfolding, a patient gathering of small moments that blossom into a vibrant, faithful life. Encouraging children to be kind, forgive freely, make good choices, cherish prayer, and trust God's timing plants enduring seeds of grace that nurture their souls beyond their years. In this sacred garden, hearts are tender, spirits are bright, and the love of God is the gentle hand that guides and sustains them all the days of their lives.

Prayer and Talking to God

What is Prayer?

Prayer is a wonderful gift, given to each of us to share our hearts and our thoughts with God. Imagine, for a moment, the brightest, most beautiful flower in a vast garden stretching as far as your eyes can see. That flower is like a prayer, unique, full of life, growing because it reaches toward the sun, which in this beautiful garden is God's love. Prayer is much like a gentle breeze that can flow quietly or a joyful song sung at the highest hills; it is the way we reach out to God, talking to Him as a dear friend, no matter where we are or what we are feeling. It is a secret path that connects your heart directly to His, allowing you to speak freely, knowing you are always heard with kindness and love, just as a child speaks to their parent or a friend shares their dreams and fears.

Sometimes, when you think about prayer, it might seem like a big, serious thing, perhaps only said in a certain way or a certain place. But in truth, prayer is as natural as breathing or laughing. It can be a quiet moment in your heart or spoken out loud in your own words. God is never too busy or too far away to listen. God wants you to talk to Him about everything, your joys, your worries, your hopes, and even your questions. Prayer is not just about asking for things; it is about sharing your day, saying thank you for the little blessings, asking for help when things are hard, or simply being still and feeling God's loving presence surround you. You don't need to use fancy words or long sentences. God listens to the language of your heart. Just like the prayers of David in the Bible, full of honesty and passion, your prayers can be a beautiful and true expression of who you are inside.

When you pray, it is important to remember that God is a good listener. Just imagine sitting with your best friend, telling them about your day, your adventures, or the times you felt scared or sad. Prayer is like that special time, except it is with the Creator of all things, the One who made the stars, the sun, the gentle rains, and you. Sometimes, you might want to say a prayer quietly before you sleep at night, asking for peaceful dreams or thanking God for the day's wonders. Other times, maybe you feel happy and want to praise God, thanking Him for laughter or friendship. Or there may be moments when your heart feels heavy with worry, and through prayer, you can lay down those burdens before Him, trusting that His love will carry you through. None of these prayers is small or unimportant. Every word spoken to God is special because it comes from you, created in His image and loved beyond measure.

It helps to know that the Bible, particularly in the King James Version, offers many beautiful words about prayer, inviting us to speak with God just as David did, pouring out his heart in songs and pleas. One such verse says, "Call unto me, and I will answer thee, and show thee great and mighty things, which thou knowest not." These words remind us that God is always ready to listen and to teach us through our prayers. When you feel uncertain what to say, it's okay to use the simple words you know, or even to sit quietly and let God fill your heart with His peace. Prayer can also be a time of listening, waiting patiently for God to speak in His gentle ways, perhaps through a feeling of warmth, a thought that brings comfort, or the light that shines softly in your mind and spirit. Prayer is a conversation, a loving dialogue between you and God, where both speaking and listening play a beautiful part.

Some children wonder if they need to use special prayers or set times to pray, but the truth is that prayer can happen anytime and anywhere. You can talk to God walking in the fields, lying in your bed, sitting under a tree, or even when your heart feels full in the middle of a noisy day. God does not mind if your words are whispered or shouted, hurried or slow; He only asks that they come honestly from your heart. Whatever you need, whether it's joy, comfort, or hope, God welcomes you always with open arms. And when you pray, you discover that your relationship with God grows stronger and more full of trust, just like a tender plant that thrives with care and attention.

Some prayers are like little seeds planted in the soil of your spirit. You might pray for someone who is sick, a friend who needs a smile, or for kindness to grow in your own heart. These prayers, though small, can blossom into powerful acts of love, inspiring you to help and care for those around you. Prayer can also teach us patience and faith, knowing that even if the answer is not quick or clear, God is working in ways we cannot see. The Bible reminds us to "Pray without ceasing," which means to keep talking to God throughout your day, sharing your thoughts and still trusting Him when you do not understand everything at once. This closeness with God through prayer becomes a living friendship, filled with hope and peace.

It is natural to ask, "How do I pray?" and the answer is simply: start anywhere. You might begin by saying, "Dear God, thank You for today," or "Please help me to be kind," or "I am sorry for the times I have made mistakes." Your words can be as simple or as long as you like. There is no perfect formula because prayer is personal, just you and God in conversation. And if you ever feel unsure or shy, you can remember that Jesus taught His friends how to pray, giving them words like, "Our Father which art in heaven, Hallowed be thy name," reminding us that God is our loving Father who hears us always. Just as children learn to talk by listening and speaking little words, so with prayer, your heart will grow in its own beautiful way as you practice daily.

Sometimes, prayers take the form of songs or poems that lift the soul to God's presence. Singing a prayer can turn a quiet moment into a joyful celebration of all the good things God has given us. Other times, prayer is a quiet whisper, a thankfulness felt deep within the heart for something as simple as a gentle rain or a warm hug. When life feels overwhelming, talking to God in prayer can feel like resting in a safe, calm harbor where you know you are never alone. Prayer is that peaceful space, created by love, where your spirit finds rest and renewal. No matter what you share in prayer, be it big or small, God listens with tender care, and His grace brightens your days.

In the stories of the children who walk with God, prayer is a joyful habit, a daily sharing of joys and worries, hopes and thanks. It is like planting tiny seeds of faith that grow into a beautiful garden of trust within their hearts. When one child prays for courage before trying something new, or another quietly thanks God for family and friends, these prayers become whispers of grace that nurture their souls. Over time, prayer becomes a natural part of their lives, a conversation that never ends. It is also a way to listen, with open hearts, to the still, small voice of God's love guiding them gently through the twists and turns of life.

Sometimes, a child may wonder if their prayers are heard when they ask for something very difficult or when they don't know what to say at all. It is important to remember that God always hears, even the silent prayers we hold within. The Bible tells us that God cares deeply for every one of His children and understands all their needs, even those too hard to put into words. When you pray with a sincere heart, you open yourself to God's grace and love, knowing that His answers may come in unexpected ways or at a perfect time known only to Him. This offering of trust is itself a kind of prayer, a beautiful song rising from the heart.

The simplest prayers can fill a day with brightness. Saying "Thank You, God" for the smiles we receive, the birds that sing, or the food we eat reminds us to notice the many small blessings around us. When you thank God in this way, prayer becomes like a joyful dance, where your heart leaps with gladness in the warmth of His love. On days when sadness clouds the sky, prayers asking for comfort can bring a quiet light to your soul, reminding you that God is close beside you, embracing you with everlasting arms.

Prayer also binds us together as friends and family. When a group of children prays together, their words rise like a sweet melody, joining hearts in hope and love. This united prayer strengthens friendships and communities, reminding us that God's love is a thread weaving us all together in kindness. No matter where children live or what language they speak, prayer is a common song, a bridge of peace built by words spoken from the heart to the One who knows us best and loves us forever.

Sometimes, prayer is a way to say sorry and ask for forgiveness, especially when we have made mistakes. Just as a gentle rain washes away dust from the leaves, prayer cleanses our hearts and helps us turn toward goodness again. The Bible teaches us that God is always ready to forgive those who seek His mercy with humble hearts. When a child prays to say sorry, it is the beginning of healing and new growth, with the promise of grace that never ends. These prayers remind us that God's love is bigger than any mistake and that He wants us to live with joy and peace once more.

Learning to pray also means learning to trust, trusting that God's love is always near, even when we cannot see it. Prayer becomes a quiet anchor in stormy times, a light in the darkness, and a song of hope rising within us. It is like whispering a secret to a friend who knows all our sorrows and joys and holds them gently in His hands. This special friendship through prayer is one of the greatest treasures we can carry in our hearts, a living connection full of warmth, kindness, and care.

Throughout the day, prayer can be like a gentle thread weaving joy into every moment. It can begin in the morning light, when you say, "God, please help me be kind today," and stretch on through the hours as you whisper quiet thanks or ask for courage when things feel tough. Before you sleep, a simple prayer of gratitude for the day's blessings can calm your heart and fill your dreams with peace. All these moments add up, creating a beautiful story of friendship with God that grows stronger and deeper, just like the roots of a mighty tree reaching down into the earth to find strength and life.

Prayer is a journey of discovering God's love anew each day. As you learn to talk to God, you also learn to listen to the still voice that soothes your fears, to the comfort that fills your soul when you feel alone, to the courage that rises when you face challenges bravely. This conversation with God invites you to share everything, trusting that you are cherished beyond words. It is a gift that lights the path ahead and fills your heart with grace, hope, and peace.

Whenever you feel ready, you might try starting your own prayer right now. It can be as simple as saying, "Dear God, thank You for loving me," or "Please help my family and friends." Remember, God delights in hearing your voice, no matter how small or shy it feels. Your prayers are seeds of grace planted in the garden of your heart, and with each one spoken in faith, love, and trust, they grow into a beautiful proof of God's eternal care. So talk to God anytime you like, just as you would a close friend, knowing you are always listened to, always loved, and never alone.

Prayers of Thanks and Sorry

Prayer is a sweet and precious way of speaking with God, like sharing your heart's deepest thoughts and feelings with your best friend, the One who loves you more than anyone else in the whole world. Children, you can pray at any time, wherever you are, and about anything inside your mind or heart. Prayer is not only for asking for help when we feel afraid or sad; it is also for sharing moments of joy, saying thank you for all the blessings, and asking forgiveness when we have made a mistake. Imagine prayer as a delicate thread that connects your soul to God's endless love, a quiet conversation that feels like a warm hug in the moments you most need comfort or courage. Every prayer, whether whispered softly or spoken aloud, is like a seed dropped into a garden, planted with hope, nurtured by faith, and blossoming into a tender exchange of love between you and your Creator.

When we think about saying thank you in our prayers, it is like opening a small treasure box in our hearts where each gift from God shines brightly. There are so many things to be grateful for: the friendly sun that wakes us in the morning, the gentle rain that helps flowers grow, the laughter of family and friends, and the kindness we share with others. Saying thank you reminds us to notice the beauty that surrounds us every day. You might pray, "Dear God, thank you for the bright blue sky and the birds that sing so sweetly. Thank you to my family who love me and for the food I eat. I am happy because you are always watching over me." This simple prayer of thanks wraps us in warmth, helping us to see that God's love is always with us, filling even the smallest moments with His gentle care and endless goodness. Words of gratitude in prayer bring light into our hearts and remind us of the many ways God paints our days with joy.

Prayers of thanks can be as big as a mountain or as small as a little seed, and both are equally beautiful to God. Sometimes, you may want to thank Him for a special moment, like a hug from someone you love or a kind word from a friend that made you smile. Other times, your prayers of thanks may be for something more general but still amazing, the gift of life itself, the stories you hear, and the wondrous world you explore each day. When you say thank you to God, it is like building a bridge of kindness and love that connects your heart to His, reminding you that no matter what happens, His good gifts never stop flowing. So do not be shy to say thanks, even for the tiniest things, because gratitude is a melody that brightens your spirit and invites more love into your life.

But sometimes, we make mistakes, we may say or do things that hurt others or displease God. These moments can make us feel sad or worried, but God's love is greater than all our mistakes. When you pray about these times, it is called asking for forgiveness. To ask for forgiveness means you are telling God you are sorry for the wrong things you have done, just like admitting to a friend when you have accidentally hurt their feelings. God listens to your prayers and welcomes your honest heart with open arms, ready to forgive and heal you. You might pray, "Dear God, I am sorry for when I was not kind to my brother or when I did not listen to my parents. Please forgive me, and help me to do better." This prayer shows courage and honesty, and it opens the door for God's grace to enter, making your heart feel light and free like a bird taking flight in the clear blue sky.

Asking for forgiveness is a way of saying that you want to grow and change, that you want to be close to God and walk in His light. It is not about feeling frightened or ashamed, but about trusting that God's mercy is bigger than anything we can imagine. When you say sorry, it is like washing away the dirt from your soul, making space for new kindness, patience, and understanding to bloom inside you. Every prayer of sorry is a fresh new beginning, a chance to learn what it means to love as God loves. It is important to remember that God forgives us always, so you can come to Him again and again, with an open heart ready to find peace and hope. This gentle cycle of asking forgiveness and receiving God's grace helps you to grow in faith, making your spirit stronger and softer at the same time.

Sometimes, it is helpful to think of prayer as a conversation made of many small moments, sometimes joyful, sometimes quiet and thoughtful, sometimes full of hope, and other times expressing sorrow. Just like you might speak differently with different friends, your prayers can take many forms. You can use your own words or the special words of the King James Bible, which are musical and beautiful, helping your heart feel close to God. You might say prayers like, "Oh Lord, I thank Thee for the gift of this day, and for the sunshine that warms my face. Forgive me, Lord, for the times I have forgotten to be kind, and help me walk in Thy ways." These words, old yet ever new, carry a sacred melody that invites peace and love to fill your soul. Using such words in your prayers can make your connection with God feel as if you are speaking in a gentle hymn, wrapped in the timelessness of His holy word.

In the stillness of the night before sleep, prayer can be a soft song of thanks and sorry, spoken in the hush of your bedroom. You might thank God for watching over you through the day and ask for forgiveness for any mistakes made. You can even ask for sweet dreams and the protection of angels beside your bed. Such prayers remind you that God is always near, guarding you with love as you rest and prepare for tomorrow. Prayer helps you remember that no matter how big or small your worries are, God holds you close. It can be as simple as whispering, "Thank You, God, for loving me so. Forgive me for my wrongs, and help me to do right." These words become a lullaby of hope and grace, helping your heart to feel safe as you drift into peaceful sleep.

At school or playtime, prayer can be like a quick secret shared with God when you need courage to be kind or strength to do what is right. When you see a friend who is sad or lonely, you might pray, "Lord, please help me to be gentle and to share a smile today." Or if you feel upset because something didn't go your way, you could say, "God, help me to be patient and forgive, just like You forgive me." These prayers, though quiet and simple, help you carry God's love with you as you journey through your day. They remind you that prayer is not only for special moments but a friend walking beside you every moment that you need.

Sometimes, prayers of thanks and sorry can be shared together, spoken with family or friends in a circle of love. Imagine gathering with those you cherish, holding hands with hearts full of hope, and saying prayers like, "Thank you, Lord, for this food and for bringing us here to share this time. Please forgive us if we have been unkind, and help us to love one another." Sharing prayer like this can make your bond with others stronger and bring a sense of peace, knowing that God hears the prayers rising like gentle birdsong from all who love Him. It becomes a special moment where love, gratitude, and forgiveness flow freely, like a river sparkling in the sunshine, refreshing everyone's souls.

Another way to pray is to think of your heart as a garden, and prayer as the rain and sunshine that help it grow. When you say thank you, it is like the sun warming the earth and helping colorful flowers bloom, flowers of joy, kindness, and love. When you say sorry, it is like the gentle rain that washes away the dust and helps new green shoots appear, shoots of goodness, patience, and hope. Prayer nourishes your spirit, encouraging the seeds of grace to sprout and blossom within you. Over time, your garden grows more beautiful, full of peace and light, becoming a place where God's love lives and flourishes. Through prayer, you become a gardener of your own heart, learning how to care for it with faith and tenderness.

Sometimes, you may wonder if your prayers are being heard or if God understands your feelings completely. The truth is, God knows your heart even better than you do because He knows all things and loves you with a love that never ends. Prayers do not need to be long or perfect; the simplest words, spoken with honesty, are most precious to Him. Whether you shout your thanks from the rooftops or whisper your sorry in a quiet moment, God's ears are always open, listening with love and kindness. Prayer is like a soft song carried on the wind, reaching the heavens where angels sing praise. Knowing this can make you feel brave and joyful, ready to talk with God anytime, trusting that He is always near and always loves you.

It is good to remember that prayer is a gift and a practice to help your spirit grow day by day. Just as you learn new things at school and play, you can learn how to pray more deeply, how to open your heart more fully, how to listen with gentle patience, and how to trust in God's perfect plan. You might write or draw your prayers, sing them like a sweet melody, or simply sit quietly and feel God's loving presence. Each way of praying helps you feel closer to Him, planting new seeds of courage, kindness, and truth within you. Prayer is an ongoing journey, a friendship that deepens as you grow, teaching you the beautiful art of grace, the magic of forgiveness, and the endless joy of saying thank you.

So dear child, never be afraid to open your heart in prayer, for God welcomes every word, every feeling, and every breath you offer. Pray with thanks when your heart is full of joy, and pray with sorry when you feel the need to ask for forgiveness. Remember that prayer is not just asking for things; it is sharing your true self with God, your hopes, your fears, your gratitude, your mistakes, and your dreams. Let prayer be the soft music that fills your days and nights, a sacred dance between you and the One who made the stars and the seas. Through prayer, may you discover the endless wellspring of God's love, flowing gently into your heart, nurturing the seeds of grace so that they may grow and bloom into a life filled with light, kindness, and peace. And always know, dear one, that you are never alone; God walks beside you, listening to your prayers, holding your hands, and loving you forever.

Listening to God

In the hush of the morning, when the world is still and the first golden rays of sun gently paint the sky, there is a sacred quietness that whispers to our hearts. It is in this quietness that we can learn to listen so very carefully, not just to the sounds around us, but to a tender voice that calls softly within. This voice belongs to God, our loving Father, who desires to speak to each one of His children, guiding their steps, comforting their fears, and filling their souls with hope and peace. Just as the gentle breeze stirs the leaves and the birds sing melodies that awaken the day, God's voice can be heard in the stillness when we choose to be very quiet and open our hearts to Him. Listening to God is a precious gift, a discovery of a secret friendship where we are never alone, and His love always surrounds us.

To begin this beautiful practice, imagine sitting in a cozy, peaceful place, a spot where the noise of the busy world grows soft. Perhaps it is a small corner of your room, or beneath the shade of a friendly tree in the garden, or even as you lay in bed just before sleep wraps you in its gentle arms. Close your eyes if you like, breathe in deep the fresh air, and let your body grow calm and still. When we draw stillness into our lives, it clears a quiet space inside, like a small pond reflecting the clear blue sky, without ripples or disturbances. This quiet place is where God's voice can be heard most clearly. Just as the clearest lake shows the purest reflection, a still heart reflects God's love and truth. It is here, in this peaceful space, that we learn to listen, not only to God's words but to His feelings, His comfort, and His guidance.

Prayer is the way we invite God to speak with us and for us to speak with Him. Think of prayer as a sweet, gentle conversation, not different from talking to a dear friend or a caring parent. It can happen at any time, when you are happy, sad, scared, or thankful. You do not need special words or fancy phrases. God listens not to how we sound, but to what is in our hearts. Prayer is simply opening your heart and saying, "Here I am, Lord," and then waiting quietly to feel His love beside you. Sometimes, when we pray, it feels as if we are the only one speaking, but in truth, God is listening with all His heart, waiting to answer in the softest of ways, a feeling of peace, a comforting thought, or a knowing that everything will be alright. When we learn to be still and listen, we begin to understand God's loving presence, even if His voice comes gently, like a whisper on the breeze.

Children often wonder how they can know that God is really listening and speaking back. It helps to remember that God's words may not sound like our parents' or teachers' voices, they are often felt as warm feelings in our hearts or as ideas that come to mind that help us do what is right and kind. God may also speak through the Bible, the beautiful book filled with His messages and stories, or through nature, in the blooming flower, the fluttering bird, or the sunshine warming our face. Sometimes God's voice comes through the gentle caring of a friend or a comforting hug from a parent. All these ways are God's tender language to us, guiding our steps as surely as a star lights the night sky for a traveler. When you listen carefully with a quiet heart, you can recognize these loving signs, and your faith grows stronger each day.

It is natural for us to feel busy and distracted, especially in a world filled with so much noise and activity. But God asks us to pause, even for a little while, and listen. Learning to be still and hear God's voice is like planting a tiny seed in the garden of your soul. At first, it may seem small or unnoticed, but with patient care, quiet moments, soft prayers, and hopeful listening, the seed will grow into a strong and beautiful tree. This tree will shelter you from troubles, give you sweet fruits of peace and joy, and stand as a sign of God's faithful love. Imagine then that each day you set aside quiet moments, just a minute or two to speak softly to God and wait with open ears and heart. Over time, you will find that listening becomes easier and prayer becomes a joyful time of friendship.

Sometimes, when we are learning to listen, our minds wander, or distractions pull us away from the quiet place inside. This is okay and quite natural. Even adults struggle to stay still and focused. What matters is the willingness to keep trying, to come back again and again to the gentle act of waiting quietly for God's words. You might find it helpful to close your eyes and breathe slowly and deeply, counting your breaths like a gentle rhythm that calms your thoughts. Another way to listen is to imagine God sitting beside you, smiling with love, holding your hand, and telling you softly that He is with you always. Just knowing this can help your heart grow peaceful and ready to hear whatever God wishes to share.

There are many beautiful prayers that can help when you want to listen to God, but even the simplest prayer spoken from your heart is precious. You might say, "Dear God, I love Thee. Please speak to me today and help me to hear Thy voice." Or, "Father, I am quiet now. Please tell me how to be kind and good." It is also wonderful to thank God in your prayers, saying what you are grateful for, such as your family, your friends, or the beautiful world around you. As you pray, remember that God delights in knowing every part of your heart, your hopes, your fears, your joys, and your sorrows. Sharing these feelings is part of listening too, for when we open our hearts fully, God's gentle answers come more clearly.

Sometimes, the voice of God will gently remind you of loving actions to take, perhaps to share a smile with someone lonely, to forgive a friend who has hurt you, or to care for a small creature that needs your help. These moments are God's way of teaching us kindness and grace. Listening to God helps us to grow in understanding how much He loves each person and wants us to live lives filled with love and goodness. When you follow God's quiet guidance, your heart feels lighter, and your spirit shines bright, lighting up your world with His love.

It is important to remember that God's love does not come only in words but in all the miracles of life around us. Each morning's sunrise, the soft petals of a flower, the laughter of a child, and the gentle rain nourishing the earth are messages from God that He cares deeply for us. When your heart listens with wonder and thankfulness, these signs speak loudly of His grace. And when you see beauty and goodness in the world, you are hearing God's voice encouraging you to be a part of His loving plan. This is the special joy of listening to God, it fills you with warmth, hope, and the courage to be loving in all you do.

The journey of learning to listen to God is one that lasts a lifetime. There will be times when His voice feels very near, and times when it seems far away. Yet, even in the quietest moments where words seem absent, God is always there, holding you close with unchanging love. You can carry this truth in your heart like a bright lamp that lights your pathway through every day. Knowing that God listens to you, and that you can listen to Him, creates a bond stronger than anything else. It is a friendship built on trust, hope, and endless kindliness, a treasure greater than gold.

You might want to share what you learn about listening with others, your family, your friends, or anyone who is learning like you. Talking about the quiet moments when you hear God's whispers helps others to find their own still places. And when you pray together, it makes your faith and friendship with God even stronger. Remember that God's voice can bring peace not only to you but to those around you. Your listening heart can become a source of kindness and light in your home and school and everywhere you go. This is a wonderful way to grow in God's love, for when we listen to Him, we also learn how to listen better to people, understanding them with patience and care.

As you continue to practice stillness and prayer, you might notice happy changes in your life. Your heart may feel softer, more forgiving, and more joyful. Challenges might not seem so big or scary because you know God walks beside you. Friendships can blossom with more kindness, and you might find yourself helping others in secret and quiet ways, guided by the gentle voice of love you hear inside. This is the treasure of listening to God, the way He shapes us into people who reflect His grace and mercy in every word and deed. You do not have to be perfect, only willing to try, to listen, and to love.

Never be afraid to speak to God about anything, for no matter how small or big your thoughts are, He always listens. If you feel lonely, angry, or confused, tell Him. If you are thankful or joyful, share your happiness with Him. Prayer is the thread that ties your heart to God's, making it stronger and more beautiful with every word. Listening to God is not something you have to do alone, it is a gentle companion walking with you, ready to share the bright light of His love whenever you are ready to hear. This friendship grows deeper with every quiet moment you spend in His presence, filling you with grace that blossoms into goodness in your daily life.

In the stillness of your heart, as you learn to listen to God, you are beginning a wonderful adventure of faith. It is a journey where every step is bathed in kindness, every challenge softened by hope, and every day brightened by the love of your Heavenly Father. So be patient with yourself, take time each day to be still, and open your heart to God's gentle whispers. Remember, the seeds of grace planted in your soul will blossom into a lifetime of peace, joy, and love, a garden tended by the hand of God

Himself. By listening, praying, and trusting, you grow closer to Him, knowing that no matter what, His voice is always near, guiding you home with tender care and everlasting faith.

The Bible, Our Guide

The Bible's Stories

Imagine a grand treasure map spread before you, its edges worn but glowing with the promise of adventure, wisdom, and wonder. This is what the Bible is, a magnificent collection of stories, poems, prayers, and teachings that have guided hearts for thousands of years. Within its pages lie treasures far more precious than gold or jewels: treasures of love, hope, courage, and faith. For every child who opens this book, it serves as a gentle and faithful companion, a daily guide through the many paths of life. Let us wander together through some of these shining stories, discovering how each one holds a special light to brighten our days and strengthen our spirits.

One of the most wondrous tales begins at the very dawn of time, when God created the world. Imagine a time before the sun warmed the earth or the rivers danced to the sea. The Bible tells us that God spoke, and by His word, light burst forth, painting the sky with the hues of dawn and dusk. Trees, flowers, birds, and animals came into being, all crafted lovingly like a master artist's brush strokes on a canvas. This story from the book of Genesis invites children to see the good and beautiful world around them as a gift, brimming with God's creative power and care. It reminds us that we, too, are part of this magnificent design, each seed and stream given purpose and praise. As you read these verses, you may feel the joy of a gentle morning breeze or hear the whisper of leaves, each a soft reminder that God's hand is ever near.

But like the turning pages of a rich tale, the story does not stop at creation's innocence. The Bible gently introduces us to another truth, sin, the sadness that came when people chose to turn away from God's perfect love. The story of Adam and Eve in the garden reminds us that even the first humans made mistakes, and like us, they faced the challenge of choosing right from wrong. Yet, even in this moment of sorrow, the narrative sings with hope. For God's love endures far beyond our stumbles. This ancient story helps children grasp that making mistakes is part of life's journey, but that forgiveness and grace always follow, like morning light after darkness.

Moving through the pages, children meet Noah, a man who trusted God when the world was very troubled. The story of the ark is a beacon of faith and obedience, teaching that in times of trial, we can cling to God's promises. Imagine the animals, two by two, entering the great wooden vessel as rain poured and the earth was washed anew. Through this tale, children learn about God's mercy and the fresh beginnings that follow when we turn back to Him. It encourages young hearts to hold fast to hope and to be kind guardians of God's creation, just as Noah cared for the creatures entrusted to him.

Another shining story is that of Joseph, a young boy who faced many hardships but never lost faith. Sold by his own brothers, he journeyed far from home, into trouble and trials. Yet, Joseph's story unfolds like a tapestry of patience, forgiveness, and divine providence. He rose from prison to palace, becoming a great helper to many, even to those who had once done him harm. This tale teaches children about resilience and kinship, the power of forgiving those who hurt us and trusting that God's plan is always working, even when we cannot see it. Joseph's coat of many colors becomes a symbol of God's promise that no matter how dark the night, dawn will surely come.

In the heart of the Bible lies the story of a shepherd boy named David, who, with a simple sling and faith in his heart, faced a giant and won. David's courage reminds children that they do not need strength or size to stand with God by their side. The story is full of bravery and trust, of a heart set on doing what is right. It also teaches about grace and repentance, as David himself made mistakes but sought forgiveness with a humble spirit. In this narrative, young readers find a friend who, like them, walked a path filled with both triumphs and trials, learning day by day to follow God's ways.

Among the most cherished stories is that of Daniel in the lion's den, where faith shines brightest in the darkest moments. Daniel's unwavering trust in God, even when faced with danger, is a lesson in bravery, honesty, and steadfast love. Imagine being surrounded by great lions, their golden eyes glowing in the dim light, yet feeling peace because God's angel watches over you. This story teaches children that God's protection surrounds those who keep their hearts faithful, and that courage born of faith can calm even the fiercest fears.

As the story of Israel's people unfolds, the Bible shares the tale of Moses, who led God's children from slavery into freedom. The great leader's journey is filled with miracles, the parting of the Red Sea, the giving of the Ten Commandments, and moments of deep conversation with God atop a mountain. Moses' story is one of obedience and trust, encouragement and challenge. Children learn that sometimes following God means stepping into the unknown, but with faith, they can be strong and brave. The Ten Commandments become a guiding light, simple rules that teach kindness, respect, and love for God and neighbor. This story soars like a great river, urging young hearts to follow the path of justice and goodness.

Turning to the words and deeds of Jesus, the Bible offers its most powerful tale of love and salvation. Jesus Christ, God's own Son, walked among people as a friend, healer, and teacher. His stories and miracles sparkle like stars in the night sky, each one bursting with lessons about kindness, forgiveness, and mercy. Jesus welcomed children, blessed the meek, and cared for the lonely, showing all how precious every soul is in God's eyes. The story of His birth in a humble manger, His life of gentle teachings, and His sacrifice on the cross remind children that God's love is the greatest treasure of all. Jesus' resurrection brings hope that life and love never end, and that all hearts can be made new. Through Jesus, the Bible speaks directly to children, inviting them into a relationship that is full of grace and joy.

Alongside Jesus' story lie the parables, short, simple tales that illustrate deep truths. Stories like the Good Samaritan, who helped a stranger in need, teach children to love their neighbors with open hands and hearts. The Prodigal Son's story offers hope that no matter how far we stray, God waits with open arms, ready to forgive and welcome us home. These parables are like gentle rivers, flowing with wisdom and urging young readers to choose kindness, patience, and mercy in their own lives.

Many stories tell of people who prayed in times of trouble, the Psalmist who sang songs of praise when feeling afraid, Hannah who prayed with all her heart for a child, and Elijah who called upon God during the silence of night. Through these moments, the Bible invites children to speak with God in their own words, trusting that He is always listening. It teaches that prayer is not just asking for help but sharing our hearts honestly, just like talking to a loving friend.

The Bible also teaches through stories that celebrate brave women of faith, like Esther, who faced danger to save her people with courage and wisdom, and Ruth, whose loyalty and kindness helped her find a new family. These stories show children that God's love and grace shine through each of us, regardless of age or place, and that we all have a role in His grand story.

As children listen to these stories, they find themselves woven into the tapestry of a mighty history, a story of a God who loves them so much that He watches over every moment of their lives. The Bible's words, especially in their King James beauty, ring with timeless melody. Phrases like "the valleys shall not be filled with darkness" or "the Lord is my shepherd; I shall not want" become lullabies and armor for the heart. These words teach children that no matter what the day holds, they are held in God's hands, nurtured by His grace.

Each story in the Bible may speak differently to every child, touching their curiosities, fears, or dreams. Some may find wonder in the animals saved on Noah's ark, others courage in David's sling, and still others refuge in the gentle teachings of Jesus. But all share the same thread, a loving God who calls them to kindness, to hope, and to faith.

By reading and remembering these stories, children cultivate seeds of grace within their hearts. They learn that they are never alone, that mistakes are but steps toward growth, and that forgiveness is always near. They come to understand that their lives, like those ancient pages, are part of a grand story, written by a God full of love, patience, and mercy. And so, with every turn of the page, every whispered prayer, and every hopeful heart, the Bible becomes not just a book, but a living garden where young spirits can bloom in truth and joy.

It is a treasure map that will guide children not only through the pages of scripture but through every adventure life may bring. It offers comfort when shadows gather, strength when the road is long, and a song of gladness that calls all young hearts to walk in the light of grace. Here, in these sacred stories, children find a friend who knows their joys and fears, who calls them by name, and who promises to be with them always. The Bible's stories are treasures indeed, rich with meaning, alive with hope, and full of the everlasting love that holds all hearts close.

God's Words for Us

In the gentle light of morning, as the world awakens with soft whispers of birdsong and the tender kiss of sunlight upon leaves, there is a special place that children can visit, a place not made of stone or wood, but of words and stories as bright and alive as the dawn itself. This place is the Holy Bible, a treasure map given by God, filled with maps through valleys, over mountains, and across seas of the heart. It is not just an ordinary book. Nay, it is a sacred guide, a loving letter sent from the heavens to every child who longs to find the path through both joyous days and shadowed nights. The Bible holds within it the many voices of God's love, speaking softly and strongly to those who seek to hear His gentle whispers in moments of happiness and times of trouble alike.

Children, imagine this: the Bible is like a garden full of shining flowers and soothing shade, a place where you can go when your heart feels full of laughter or when tears have found their way like gentle rain. The words within the Scriptures are gifts, shining lamps in the darkness, guiding feet that sometimes falter on rocky roads. When we are happy, the Bible rejoices with us; when we are sad or afraid, it brushes kindness over our souls and assures us we are never alone. The Scriptures are alive, breathing hope and courage into every page, ever ready to tell the children of the world that love, grace, and peace are closer than a heartbeat away.

In the pages of the King James Bible, you will find stories of people who were just like you, children and grown-ups who laughed and played under the same sun, who worried as you might worry, and who discovered marvelous truths about God's love. There is King David, a shepherd boy who trusted God's protection when giants loomed large, teaching us that even the smallest among us can be strong with faith. There is the tender story of Ruth, who chose kindness and loyalty when the path was uncertain, showing us that love holds us steady even in the hardest times. And there is the beautiful journey of Jesus Christ, who walked among the lilies and the hills, speaking words of forgiveness, healing, and eternal hope. These stories are like sparkling stars in a vast night sky, lighting the way for young hearts to understand the great and loving character of God.

But more than stories, the Bible is a treasure trove of sacred words, verses and promises that speak directly to each child's soul. When you feel lonely, you can turn to the Psalmist who wrote, 'The Lord is my shepherd; I shall not want.' This means God watches over you like a loving shepherd watching over little sheep, leading you to green pastures where you are safe and cared for. When sadness clouds your heart, the words of Jesus offer comfort, saying, 'Come unto me, all ye that labour and are heavy laden, and I will give you rest.' Here, Jesus invites all those who feel tired or troubled to come near Him to find peace as gentle as a mother's embrace. These verses are like gentle friends who walk beside you, reminding you deep inside that God's love never fails or fades.

Sometimes, children face challenges that seem too big to bear, a misunderstanding with a friend, a lost pet, a scary night, or feelings of worry about school or family. At such times, the Bible's words become a balm of peace. They teach children how to pray, talking to God just as you would to a friend, sharing gladness, asking for help, and learning to listen for answers whispered softly in the quiet of the heart. When the world feels loud and confusing, the Bible offers stillness, a quiet haven where young souls can rest and be renewed. In those moments, the verses weave a tapestry of promise and strength, such as the words found in Isaiah that say, 'Fear thou not; for I am with thee: be not dismayed; for I am thy God.' These words remind children that they carry a mighty protector in their hearts, a God who never leaves and who is always near.

The Bible also teaches kindness and forgiveness, guiding children in how to love others and themselves. It shows us that grace, the beautiful gift of God's unearned love, is like a seed planted deep inside that grows into flowers of patience, gentleness, and joy. The words 'Be ye kind one to another, tenderhearted, forgiving one another, even as God for Christ's sake hath forgiven you' encourage children to be gentle friends who lift each other up rather than pull each other down. In this way, the Bible helps children to build hearts full of love, teaching them that forgiveness is not only a gift from God but a way to make the world brighter for everyone.

When troubles come like storms and the nights stretch long, the Bible's words act as a lantern in the dark. Through King Solomon's wisdom, we learn that 'Trust in the Lord with all thine heart; and lean not unto thine own understanding.' This teaches children that when we face puzzles too big for our minds to solve, we can rest in knowing God's wisdom is greater than anything else. The Bible does not promise that life will be easy, but it does promise that God's love will never leave us alone in our struggles. It's like a strong hand held in the darkest valley, always ready to lift us up when we fall.

Throughout the year, when seasons change and new adventures await, God's words remain a steady song, sung softly over the days and nights. They teach children about the blessings found in faith and the joy that blooms when hearts trust in God's goodness. Like the words from the gospel of John, 'For God so loved the world, that he gave his only begotten Son, that whosoever believeth in him should not perish, but have everlasting life,' the Bible shares the most wondrous promise of all, that no matter what happens, God's love reaches out to all people, young and old alike, inviting everyone into a life full of hope and light.

Children learn from the Bible that they are special in God's eyes, each a precious treasure lovingly created and cared for. The Bible says, 'I have called thee by thy name; thou art mine.' This tender assurance reminds children that God knows their names, their dreams, and even their fears. He is never too busy or far away to listen to the laughter or the tears that spill from a small heart. And whenever days seem dark or heavy, children can open their treasured Bible, and hear God's voice whispering through the sacred words, saying, 'Peace I leave with you, my peace I give unto you: not as the world giveth, give I unto you.' These words offer a loving calm that no storm can shake, a divine comfort that fills the soul like warm sunshine after a long rain.

Using the Bible as a daily guide is like carrying a shining compass wherever one may roam. When feeling joyful, the Bible invites children to thank God with songs of praise and to share their happiness with friends and family. When feeling scared or upset, the Bible becomes a quiet friend, helping children to pray and find courage in God's promises. It teaches that no matter the circumstance, whether walking through sunny meadows of delight or trudging through shadowed valleys of doubt, God's words remain a steadfast light, helping every step be strong and sure.

Even the simplest verse can be a powerful seed planted in a child's heart, growing tall and firm over time. Verses like 'Children, obey your parents in the Lord: for this is right' show the way to live in harmony at home with love and respect. Other verses, like 'Love thy neighbour as thyself,' open children's eyes to the beauty of kindness and caring for others, a shining thread weaving hearts together in the fabric of God's family. As children learn these verses, they begin to see how God's word is not only for quiet moments but for every step of their daily lives, at school, at play, and at rest.

Parents and caregivers, too, find joy in sharing these sacred verses with children, creating moments of wonder and growth. Together, as the Bible's words are shared softly and lovingly, families build a bond deeper than words, a bond knitted with faith and hope, with trust and forgiveness. In these shared times, children feel wrapped in the warmth of God's love, their souls blossoming like the lilies of the field that neither toil nor spin but are clothed with beauty from God's own hand. This tender nurturing helps children grow strong in faith and kind in heart, ready to face the world gently but boldly.

Sometimes children ask why the Bible's language sounds different, with words like 'thee' and 'thou,' like a song from a faraway land. This timeless beauty is like a melody that has traveled through centuries, echoing the majesty and holiness of God. It is a special way of speaking that invites children to step into a sacred story not just of people long ago, but of eternal truth that still breathes and lives today. Understanding a little of this language helps children feel connected to a great cloud of witnesses, the many faithful souls who have read, loved, and leaned on these words for thousands of years. It is a legacy of love, a heritage of hope, handed down like a precious jewel.

And so, dear child, whenever life feels bright or shadows creep near, remember that the Bible is like a treasure map, carefully guiding your heart with the sparkling gems of God's words. It holds stories of goodness and grace, of forgiveness and courage, waiting for you to discover and carry with you wherever you go. Let its words be your friends, always ready to cheer you, comfort you, and remind you that you are loved beyond measure. In the embrace of these sacred verses, may your soul find rest, your spirit grow strong, and your heart bloom in the everlasting grace of God's tender love.

Reading Together

There is a special magic that happens when voices rise together around the gentle pages of an open Bible, like a sweet melody weaving comfort and light within the hearts gathered close. Imagine the Bible not merely as a book, but as a treasure map unfolding before your eyes, a map etched in the language of the King James Bible, full of stories shining like stars in the night, lessons whispered like the wind through ancient trees, and promises resting like sparkling jewels upon the paths we journey. When you and your family open this wondrous book, you do not simply read words; rather, you set sail upon a grand adventure, exploring the meadows of goodness, the valleys of heartfelt sorrow, and the mountains of hope and joy. Within these treasured stories, each syllable holds a treasure to discover, a seed of grace ready to be planted in your tender heart.

Reading together begins with a whisper, sometimes soft as a lullaby, inviting all to join in the dance of words that float like birds aloft, each one carrying messages written by a voice older than time itself. The King James Bible speaks with a rhythm and melody that even children can feel, its sacred phrases flow like gentle rivers, touching the shores of your imagination and painting pictures more vivid than any artist's brush.

When a mother or father reads aloud to a child, or brothers and sisters gather in a close circle, these words become bridges, connecting stories told in ages long past to the laughter and tears shared in the light of today's hearth. In the shining eyes of children, the tale of Adam and Eve in Eden springs to life not as a dusty tale, but as a vibrant dance of innocence, choice, and consequence, teaching them about the wonder of God's creation and the tender grace that follows the mistakes we make.

The act of reading aloud these stories of love and learning is itself a blessing, for it creates a sacred space where the warmth of voices mingles with the quiet strength of the scriptures. Each story gently unwraps the lessons hidden within, the meaning of sin as not just a distant concept but a shadow we all wrestle with, and the wonderful hope of salvation as a light breaking forth over the horizon, brighter than the clearest dawn. As the words roll forth, the subtle cadences of the King James Bible invite children to listen not only with their ears but with their hearts, drawing them ever closer into a world where forgiveness flows like an endless river and kindness blossoms even in the most tender and fragile soil.

Encouraging children to share these stories with family brings life to the pages in a way that reading silently cannot. Always there is a child's laugh or a silent sigh, a thoughtful pause or a question that springs like a fresh stream from the well of curiosity. When a child asks, "What does this mean?" or softly wonders, "Why would God forgive such a big mistake?" it becomes a doorway to deeper discovery, a chance for the family to gather even more tightly around the warmth of faith. Together, parents and children can explore the mysteries of grace, how the Savior's love, so vast and endless, touches each soul no matter the size of the wrong done or the trembling doubt that might flicker within. It is in these moments of shared exploration that the Bible becomes not just a book to read, but a living companion, a guide through the winding roads of life, holding hands firmly with each reader, whispering encouragement and peace.

Families who read the scriptures together weave a tapestry of memory and meaning, stitching the golden threads of God's promises into the very fabric of their days. The stories, whether they tell of David's courage facing the giant, or Jesus's gentle healing touch, or the quiet prayers of the Psalmist, carry the power to shape the hearts of children, instilling in them a sense of belonging and a knowledge that love, mercy, and grace are theirs to know and share. These moments of reading also plant the knowledge that God's words are a lamp unto the feet, a light unto the path, guiding each step with clarity and hope, especially when the world feels dark or confusing.

Sharing Bible stories at home becomes a precious ritual, a sanctuary of moments set apart from the busy hum of daily life. Perhaps as the evening sun dips behind the hills and shadows grow long, a family gathers in the soft flicker of candlelight or beside a glowing hearth. Hands may be held, heads softly bowed, as voices rise in unison, echoing scriptures like a lullaby to the soul. Or in the morning's fresh hush, reading aloud becomes a song of promise, a prayerful beginning filled with courage for the day ahead. These shared readings comfort and encourage, binding family members with invisible cords woven from faith and hope. They teach children not only the stories but the sacred rhythms of prayer, reflection, and gratitude that are part of a life woven with God's presence.

Long after the voices fall silent, the seeds planted in these times of reading together take root, growing in gardens of the heart where kindness blooms and grace waters every leaf. When children hear the King James Bible's timeless phrases like "For God so loved the world," or "Though I walk through the valley of the shadow of death, I will fear no evil," they absorb comfort and strength not only for the page but for moments beyond, when they might feel alone or afraid. Such words gently remind them that the greatest of friends walks beside them always, that forgiveness is not just a tale told but a gift offered anew each day. The power of shared reading lies in its ability to knit the family together in these truths, creating a heritage of faith that children carry forward into all their tomorrows.

Parents and caregivers play a precious role as guides through this joyful journey. They become storytellers of God's love, interpreters of the sacred text, unraveling complex stories into strands children can hold gently, like smooth stones found by a quiet brook. With patience and tenderness, they explain that sin is real but not a final sentence, that mistakes are invitations to learn and grow rather than marks of failure. They show how Jesus Christ is the bridge over which all may safely cross, offering grace unfathomable and forgiveness that restores wholeness to every heart willing to receive it. In this, reading together becomes an act of love, a nightly gift offering safety, wisdom, and hope that will nurture children long beyond the last story told.

At times, reading together might invite questions and reflections that surprise even the grown-ups, prompting new collections of prayers, thoughts, and dreams spoken into the warmth of the family circle. A child may wonder why God allows hardship or what it means to have faith. These moments are like stars in the dark, guiding all toward deeper understanding and closer bonds. Together, family members can explore the many colors of God's character, His justice, mercy, and tender kindness, and see how these attributes shine through each story. With each shared reading, the King James Bible's rich language wraps itself softly around the child's developing soul, teaching reverence and beauty alongside truth and wisdom.

Frequently, families discover that reading scripture aloud awakens not only understanding but also a love for these ancient words, encouraging children to turn again and again to the Bible's pages. Soon, the book becomes a treasured companion, its stories recalled with joy and its lessons carried quietly throughout the day's play and rest. The cadence of the King James Bible, with its noble and poetic voice, lingers in the imagination like a gentle song, strengthening faith's roots and offering a peaceful refuge amid life's hurried moments. Children begin to recognize familiar passages, sometimes repeating the words in their play or whispering them softly like a prayer when they feel alone. This beautiful intertwining of language, story, and spirit is the heart's blessing, born from simply reading and sharing God's Word together.

Furthermore, reading the Bible as a family cultivates gratitude and mindfulness, guiding children to see the world through the lens of love and care. As they hear stories of creation's beauty, of the faithful courage of biblical heroes, and of Jesus's boundless compassion, children learn that their own lives are part of this grand story. They come to understand that just as God worked through Moses, David, and Mary, so too does God's love move quietly in their own home, in each kind word, every act of forgiveness, every shared smile. The scriptures become mirrors reflecting their own journeys, and through reading together, families build a shared language of faith and hope that stretches far beyond the pages.

To nourish this growing love of Scripture, families might discover treasures in the act of retelling stories in their own words, drawing pictures inspired by the sacred scenes, or gently praying together for the strength to live with kindness and grace. The Bible's stories invite all to come close, to linger, to ask and to share. Through such gentle engagement, children learn that faith is not static but a vibrant, living relationship, a friendship with God that flows naturally from the shared discovery of His Word. The family reading becomes a garden where seeds of faith and understanding are sown, nurtured by shared laughter, tears, and whispered dreams.

It is also wonderful to recognize that reading the Bible together does not have to be perfect or formal; it is the spirit of gathering, the act of turning pages together, that matters most. Whether it is a quiet moment before sleep or a daily pause at the breakfast table, the precious time spent connecting with God's Word becomes a wellspring of peace and belonging. In this gentle rhythm, children grow to know that no matter where life's path leads, they are loved and guided by a Father whose voice has echoed through centuries yet speaks as tenderly today as ever. The King James Bible's words, so grand and true, provide steady footsteps along the way, and every family gathering to read becomes a beacon shining softly with hope.

Together, as families share these ancient yet ever-new stories, the King James Bible's timeless wisdom becomes the lantern carried through all of life's seasons, lighting up the dark, warming the cold, and guiding every step with grace. Children learn that the Bible is a gift lovingly given, meant to be read aloud, treasured closely, and lived out in kindness and faith. Thus, through the simple but wondrous act of reading together, hearts are knit lovingly into God's eternal story, and the seeds of grace take firm root, ready to bloom in the bright, shining garden of a child's life.

Faith as a Journey

Planting Faith

In the quiet kingdom of the earth, beneath the soft blanket of soil where the light does not reach, a tiny seed lies resting. It is small and seemingly powerless, hardly the kind of thing you would think could grow into something mighty and strong. Yet, within this little seed lies a miracle of life waiting to unfold. Just as the seed is hidden away, waiting patiently for its moment to emerge, so too does faith begin its gentle journey deep inside a young heart. At first, faith is a whisper, barely noticed, a quiet hope that shines softly like the glow of early dawn. It does not burst forth in grandeur or make a sudden splash, but grows slow and sure, faithfully watered by moments of kindness, curious questions, and gentle prayers.

In the beginning, a seed knows nothing but the cold embrace of the earth. It feels the dampness and the pressure all around, challenging its tiny spirit to awaken. So must faith endure the seasons of doubt and questions, the days when the heart feels uncertain and the path seems unclear. These moments are like a winter's chill upon the soil, seemingly harsh and unwelcoming. Yet, beneath the surface, change stirs unseen, for the seed's husk softens, and new life stirs within. In much the same way, when a child looks up at the night sky full of stars and wonders about God, this is the silent stirring of faith beginning to stretch its roots. It may feel small or fragile, but it is real and growing, hidden in the soil of the heart.

Water is the seed's greatest friend. With each drop, the seed swells and softens, drawing strength from the kindness of the rain. Without water, it remains dry and silent, unable to reach out toward the sun. Faith too must be watered with love, soft words from a parent, a story told from the Bible, or a quiet moment spent in prayer. These gentle acts pour over the spirit, nourishing a tender trust that God is near, watching over each child. Just as a gardener patiently tends the earth, so must children and their caregivers patiently nurture faith. Sometimes the growth is slow and unseen, and sometimes faith seems to falter, but the quiet care continues without cease. Each prayer, each act of kindness, each heartfelt question is like a gentle rain upon the soul.

As the seed grows roots, it finds strength in the soil, reaching deep to hold firm against the winds and storms. Roots are like the foundation of faith, the knowledge that God's love is steady and unchanging, no matter the troubles life may bring. The roots do their quiet work day after day, holding the plant safe so that the stem might rise upward. Children learn this foundation through stories of God's promises, the gentle words of Jesus speaking of love and forgiveness, and the many ways God cares for His creation. When a child feels safe in this knowledge, faith is rooted deeply, enabling courage and hope to grow tall. The roots that grow quietly under the earth are unseen but mighty, just as the quiet trust in God is a power within the heart.

When the first green shoot breaks through the earth, it is a moment of wonder. The seed that once seemed so small and hidden now reaches toward the sun, thirsty for light and warmth. Just so does faith begin to show itself in actions and choices. Every small act of kindness, every "thank you" to God, every moment of forgiveness is like a leaf unfolding to the heavens. The light of God's love pours down like the warm sun, encouraging faith to grow even stronger. But even then, the young sprout must bend to the wind and weather the rain; it is not always easy to grow. Sometimes faith feels fragile or uncertain in the face of hard questions or when the world seems confusing. Yet with God's light shining steadily, patience and trust hold fast, and growth continues.

Growth takes time and cannot be rushed. Just as the gardener knows not to pull at the sprout to force it taller, children learn that faith is not something hurried but something cherished and respected in its own season. A child's belief may start small, a quiet thought of God's goodness at night, or a simple hope that things will be better. These beginnings may seem silent and small, but they are precious. God delights in these tender moments of trust and watches with joy as faith stretches higher bit by bit. Spiritual growth is like watching a garden in spring, where bulbs crack the frozen ground and colorful flowers slowly bloom. It is not a race but a journey, filled with wonder and surprises along the way.

Care for faith is an act of love, like the rain and sunshine caring for the growing plant. It is found in daily conversations about God's word, the sharing of stories from the Bible, and the quiet times spent with Jesus in prayer. Children learn that just as a plant needs air to breathe and nutrients from the soil, faith requires attention and practice. Talking to God, listening to His voice in the heart, and choosing kindness are all ways of nurturing the soul. It is in these small, repeated acts that faith gains strength to stand firm. When a child chooses to forgive a friend or to share a smile with someone who is sad, these moments water faith's roots and encourage branches of love to grow outward.

Trust in God's timing is as important as care. A seed does not know how long it must lie beneath the soil before the sun will warm it just so. It cannot rush the sunrise or force the rain to fall. It simply rests in patient hope. Similarly, children learn that God's plans unfold in their own perfect time. Sometimes the heart longs for answers or wonders when faith will become strong and bright. The story of the seed is a reminder that God's timing is perfect and that faith grows slowly, day by day, sometimes in sunshine and sometimes in storm. Every season serves a purpose; every moment of waiting holds a promise. In this way, faith becomes a quiet companion, whispering gently: "Be patient, for the Lord's hand is guiding thee."

As faith grows, it becomes not just a seed hidden in the soil, but a tree strong enough to shelter others. It is like a mighty oak offering shade to those who seek refuge on a hot day. When a child's faith takes root and grows tall, it is a gift not only for themselves but for their family, friends, and community. Acts of kindness born from faith ripple outward like branches stretching wide. Love and grace flow freely, touching hearts beyond their own. The small seed that once seemed so frail becomes a forest of hope and strength. This is the promise that faith carries, a journey from a tiny whisper of trust to a mighty chorus of praise and love.

And so, the story of faith is a story of beginning small and growing big, just as the little seed becomes a strong and towering tree. It teaches children that their faith, no matter how quiet or simple it starts, is precious and alive, fed by care, watered by love, and strengthened by patience. It reminds them to trust God's gentle hand, for He is the Gardener of hearts and souls. As they watch the seedling become a tree, they learn that faith is a treasure worth nurturing, a gift that blooms forever in the garden of life. Each small step of belief, each prayer whispered softly in the night, is a promise that God's grace is watching over them, gently guiding their growth, until one day they stand tall and strong, full of hope, love, and peace.

Watering with Prayer

In the quiet moments of dawn, when the first light gently brushes the earth, a little seed lies beneath the soil, waiting patiently to grow. It is small and unseen, but within it, life stirs. Just as this tiny seed requires water to awaken and rise, so too does our faith need a special kind of watering, a watering with prayer. Prayer is like the gentle rain that falls softly from the heavens, refreshing our hearts and helping our belief in God to blossom. It is one of the most tender and important ways we can care for the small seeds of faith planted inside each one of us.

Faith, much like a seed in the dark earth, often begins in quiet places within us, places we may not even notice at first. We can feel a warmth, a gentle stirring of hope and trust deep inside our hearts, even if we do not yet fully understand what it means. When we take a moment to speak to God through prayer, it is as if we are sending a loving invitation to Him, telling Him we would like to grow closer and learn from His endless love. Prayer is not just about asking God for what we want, though He does listen and cares deeply; it's about sharing our feelings, our hopes, and even our fears, trusting that He is near and ready to nurture us in His perfect way and perfect time.

Imagine a bright, clear morning on a garden path. A gardener understands that seeds do not sprout and bloom in a single burst. They need constant care: the right amount of sunshine, the gentle touch of rain, and the patience to watch and wait. Without these things, the seed remains silent and still, unable to reach for the sky. In the same way, our faith needs continuous care, gently watered by prayer. Every time we bow our heads and speak softly or silently to God, we are watering our spiritual seed. It may seem small or slow at first, and sometimes we might not see any change, but God is always at work, nurturing us in ways we cannot always see.

Prayer is the lifeline that connects us to God's loving presence. It is a special gift He gave us so that we can open our hearts freely and honestly, without fear or hesitation. In prayer, we find a safe place, a quiet corner of the soul where we can rest and be understood. Sometimes, when sadness or confusion creeps into our lives like a dark cloud, prayer becomes the rain that washes away our worries and replaces them with peace and hope. Other times, prayer is the soft illumination of sunshine that warms us and reminds us we are not alone, that God's love is like the brightest light guiding our steps through the world.

Children, when you pray, you are watering a tiny seed inside you that will grow and grow, stretching upward like a tall tree reaching for the sky. Just as a seedling must push through the earth's tough cover before it can see the sunlight, your faith sometimes must grow quietly and patiently. Prayer helps your confidence and trust in God grow stronger each day. It reminds you that even when things are hard, or when you feel scared or lonely, God is with you, listening, holding you close, and giving you strength.

Many times, the most wonderful things in life happen slowly. Like the seasons turning one into another, faith grows over time as you pray, listen, and learn to trust God's gentle guidance. Sometimes, you may wonder why it takes so long for your prayers to be answered or how the little seed inside you can become strong enough to face life's challenges. Remember, the kingdom of God grows not with rushing, but with steady love and care. Just as you would not pull on a fragile sprout to make it grow faster, only risking harm, you do not need to hurry your faith. God knows your heart and is patiently and lovingly helping you grow exactly when and how you need.

Prayer also teaches us to listen, to be quiet and still enough to hear God's voice. In our busy days, it can be hard to find moments of calm. But when we stop to pray, it is not only our words that matter; it is the stillness we create that allows God's whispers of love and wisdom to reach us. It is in this sacred conversation, this gentle watering of our souls, that our faith is nurtured and strengthened. God speaks in many ways, in the laughter of a friend, the beauty of a sunset, or the kindness of a stranger, and when we pray, we create space for these blessings to bloom in our hearts.

As children open their eyes in the morning and thank God for the new day, they practice prayer's beautiful gift of gratitude. Saying thank you for small things, the warmth of the sun, a hug from a parent, the sweetness of a song, plants seeds of joy and contentment deep within. Gratitude, watered by prayer, grows into a rich garden of hope, reminding us that God's goodness is always around us, even when we cannot see it at once. By watering your heart with thanks, you invite God's grace to fill you, making your faith tree stand tall and strong.

Prayer is also a way to ask God for help, to say, "I am sorry," when we have made mistakes, and "Please help me," when we feel afraid or unsure.

Just as a seedling might lean heavily on a support stake to grow upright in the wind, our prayers for mercy and strength help us stand firm through life's storms. No one is perfect, not even the tallest tree or the most lovely flower. We all have times when we stumble or fall, but prayer reconnects us to God's forgiving hands. It reminds us that no matter what happens, God's love is the safest place to rest, to heal, and to find courage to try again.

There is a special kind of magic in prayer that children can feel deep in their bones, a warmth that hushes worries and fills the soul with gentle peace. It is like the soft wind that carries seeds across fields or the morning dew that sparkles on tender leaves. The magic is not in complicated words or perfect voices, but in the pure and simple act of speaking from the heart and trusting that God is listening. Sometimes, prayers are whispered like a secret, sometimes sung like a joyful song, and sometimes felt as a quiet hope. Each one waters the seed of faith, helping it break through the soil and grow into something beautiful and strong.

Every day, as you breathe and live, you can water your seed of faith just by remembering God and saying a little prayer. It can be as small and sweet as "Thank You, God," before you eat your food, or "Please help me be kind," when you are feeling upset. These little prayers, like delicate drops of rain, gather together to nourish your spirit and bring about a joyful bloom. Over time, these prayers fill your heart with confidence that God is always near, guiding your steps and filling your life with love and grace.

Children learning to pray also learn to trust in God's timing, which is not always the same as theirs. Just like the seed does not grow overnight, answers to prayers sometimes take days, weeks, or even years to appear. God's ways are wondrous and wise, much beyond what we can fully understand, but they are always for the best. When you wait patiently with faith, like a gardener watches over their tender plants, you learn that God's perfect timing brings the most beautiful blossoms. Sometimes, a prayer's answer comes softly as a kind word from a friend, or as a gentle peace that calms your heart, even when all seems uncertain.

By praying, children also join a vast family of believers who have nurtured their own seeds of faith through every generation. Long ago, people like Abraham, Moses, and David prayed with trust and hope, even when their journeys were hard. Jesus, too, prayed often, speaking to His Father God and teaching His friends to do the same. When you pray, you step into this great cloud of witnesses, standing side by side with those who have come before you, all growing and learning in God's love. This connection gives strength and courage, reminding you that prayer is a timeless gift, ever strong and true.

Prayer also invites you to share your yearnings for kindness and goodness not just for yourself but also for others. When you pray for your family, friends, or even those you do not know well, you water the seeds of love and compassion in your heart. You learn that faith is not just something that grows quietly inside but also a light that shines outward, warming the lives of those around you with grace and mercy. Through prayer, your faith reaches roots beyond yourself, touching the world in ways big and small.

Remember, watering your seed with prayer does not depend on having perfect words or knowing exactly what to say. Prayer is a conversation full of love, a precious moment when your heart speaks freely to God, and God's love speaks back to you. You do not have to be alone to pray; God is always near, ready to listen. Sometimes you can close your eyes and whisper, sometimes you can sing, or even simply sit in silence, feeling God's gentle presence. No matter how you pray, it is the watering of your spirit that encourages your faith to grow tall and strong.

In closing, dear children, think of prayer as the most tender and faithful gardener of your soul's garden. Every word you speak to God is like a drop of rain, every moment you spend listening is like sunlight gently warming your leaves, and every breath of hope is like the fresh air that helps you stretch your branches toward the heavens. As you continue to water your seed with prayer, with patience and love, your faith will grow into a magnificent tree, a tree of trust, kindness, and joy that stands strong through all seasons, rooted deep in God's everlasting love. And like the trust that a seed places in the earth and the rain, you too are held safely in God's hands as you grow, blossom, and shine with grace.

Growing Strong and Tall

In the quiet whisper of the garden, beneath the rich and tender earth, a seed lies waiting. Small and unassuming, it holds within it the promise of a mighty tree yet to come, though none outside the soil can guess its destiny. So too is the faith of a child, hidden deep within the heart, filled with potential, yet needing time, care, and patience to unfold. Just as the seed must patiently endure the dark and damp, the seasons and the storms before it stretches forth its arms toward the sun, so does a young heart grow strong through trials and tender nurturing, through moments of doubt and times of joy, trusting that God's hand gently guides the process in His perfect time.

To grow strong and tall is not something that happens swiftly or without care. It is a journey marked by persistence, much like the seed pushing through the soil with quiet determination. The earth does not rush the seed, nor does the seed rise hurriedly to the sky; instead, there is a slow and steady unfolding, a delicate reaching that carries it upwards. Young hearts, too, can learn from the steadfast patience of the seed. When moments of waiting feel long or when troubles blow like fierce winds against the tender sprout, it is trust in God's plan that fortifies the spirit. In these times, children are invited to remember the promises whispered through sacred texts: that the Lord watches over His creation, that He tends His children with unfailing love, and that every step forward, no matter how small, is part of a divine blossoming.

There is beauty in every phase of growth, whether it be in the heart of a seedling or the journey of a child learning faith. Each inch gained is evidence of life taking hold, of roots growing deep into the soil, anchoring firmly against the storms. Like the young tree that bends but does not break when the wind blows, so too must a child learn to hold fast to the steady truth of God's word. Sometimes faith may appear fragile, bending beneath the weight of questions or the cool shadow of uncertainty, but it is never broken. For God's grace is like the sun's warm rays, steadfast and sure, giving the strength to stand tall once more.

Imagine a seed beneath the earth sensing the stirrings of life around it. Slowly it pushes upward, breaking through the darkness into the light, turning itself toward the warmth of the sun. Its growth is humble and slow, but mighty in its perseverance. So the young heart begins to see the wonders of God's creation, to feel the touch of His love spread within, and to understand that even the smallest act of kindness, the gentlest prayer, and the softest whisper of hope are like rays of sunlight helping faith grow. Each day brings the chance to trust a little more, to wait a little longer, and to believe a little deeper that God's plan is unfolding in perfect wisdom.

Trust in God's plan is like the unseen roots anchoring a tree deep into the earth. Though they remain hidden, these roots hold the tree steady and nourish it with water and life. So does faith reach beneath the surface of what the eye can see, grounding a child in the knowledge of a loving Creator. When days are sunny and joyful, it is easy to feel close to God, like leaves basking in warm light. But even in moments of shadow or storm, the roots of faith grow stronger, for they draw from a source that never fades. In the quiet times of prayer, in the times of reading scripture, and in gentle acts of kindness, these roots deepen and spread, making possible the magnificent growth of grace and strength that stands the test of time.

Growing strong is not about the size of the tree, nor how swiftly it reaches the sky. It is about the steady unfolding of life, marked by faithful steps and trust in the One who made the seed. Just as a tree may take years before it bears fruit, so must a child's faith be tended with patience and love. Each lesson learned, each prayer lifted, and each act of forgiveness is a drop of rain, a sunbeam, or a gentle breeze that encourages growth. Sometimes progress feels unseen, hidden beneath seasons when nothing appears to happen, but the promise remains sure, growth is always underway, just as the seed rises unseen toward the light, gathering strength and preparing to bloom.

Children can take heart in the story of growth, knowing that the Lord is their gardener. His care is gentle and His timing perfect, slower than their hurried wishes perhaps, but filled with wisdom far greater than any they know. When discouragement creeps in, or impatience whispers softly, they may hold tightly to this truth: growth is a story written in faith, and every season has its purpose. Like a tree rooted deeply despite storms, their hearts will stand strong if they trust. Day by day, through prayer and kindness, through learning and loving, the Spirit nurtures the seed of faith, watering it, guiding it, until it rises tall and proud to testify to the goodness of God.

The story of becoming strong and tall is beautifully simple in its teaching yet profound in its reach. It asks children to imagine themselves as that tiny seed, small, tender, but filled with the promise of greatness in God's hands. It reminds them that growth requires patience, that setbacks are not endings but parts of the journey, and that trust is the invisible force that carries them forward. When doubts come, when the path seems tangled, or the sun hides behind clouds, the child is gently encouraged to look within, to pray to God who knows every beat of their heart, and to remember that they are never alone. For the One who called the seed to grow also calls each child to flourish in His grace.

Faith, like a growing tree, is a slow and wondrous unfolding. It is painted not only in the stretches toward heaven but also in the unseen stretches of roots that keep it grounded. This teaches the young reader that becoming a person of grace and strength is more than shining brightly in the sun, it is also about standing firm in trials, reaching out with hope beyond what is seen, and trusting the One who holds all things in His hands. As they grow strong and tall in spirit, their lives become a living testament to the power of God's love, a shade for others seeking refuge, and a home for kindness to flourish abundantly.

In the quiet moments before sleep, as a child's thoughts drift softly like the gentle breeze through leaves, they may feel the tender assurance that growth is part of a grand design. The King James Bible speaks with a voice both ancient and alive, telling stories that ripple like rivers through the soul. These words offer a gentle invitation: be patient, be faithful, and know that God's timing is perfect. Like a seed that must wait for the right moment to blossom, every child's heart will bloom in its own time, becoming strong and tall, a living sign of the grace that covers them and of the eternal hope planted deep within.

Therefore, dear child, when you feel small and unsure, remember the seed beneath the earth, the tiny promise cradled in dark soil, unseen but never forgotten. Trust in God's plan, who watches over you with tender eyes and a loving heart. Let your faith grow in quiet hope, in steady perseverance, and gentle trust, knowing that your journey is guided by the hand that formed the heavens and the earth. Grow strong and tall in grace, for you are a beloved child of God, ever-growing in His everlasting love.

A Heart Full of Grace

Grace is a Gift

Grace is a Gift, a wondrous, shining gift that flows not from anything we earn or deserve, but from the boundless heart of God Himself. Imagine the brightest light, spreading warmth and peace to all the dark corners of the world; that light is grace. It is a tender embrace offered to us before we speak a word or take a single step, a love so deep and wide that it covers every mistake, so gentle and strong that it lifts us when we stumble. To understand grace is to open our hearts to a treasure beyond gold or jewels, a precious gift wrapped not in silver or silk, but in the endless kindness of God's spirit, given freely and fully to every one of His children. We have traveled together through stories and lessons, walking through the gardens of innocence and the valleys shadowed by sin, and now we stand at the doorstep of grace itself, a place where all those journeys find their meaning and hope.

In the beginning, when Adam and Eve walked in the beautiful garden of Eden, they lived in perfect harmony with God's creation, pure and unafraid. Yet with choice came the shadow of sin, the breaking of that harmony, and the beginning of humanity's need for grace. From that very moment, God's grace began to weave its way into the story of humanity, a promise whispered gently through the leaves and carried on the winds, a promise that though we may fall, we are never beyond the reach of His love. Grace is what God offers to us when we fail, when we are small and broken and unsure, inviting us not just to stand again but to grow stronger, kinder, and wiser, guided by His everlasting light. It is easy sometimes to think that love and kindness must be earned by good deeds alone, but grace teaches us a different truth, that we are loved first, cherished always, and that love changes us from the inside out.

To embrace grace is to accept this great gift, to let it fill our hearts with warmth and hope even on the coldest days. It is a choice to forgive ourselves as God forgives us, not counting our wounds or mistakes as burdens, but as steps along the path toward becoming better, more loving children of God. In the stories of Jesus Christ, we see grace made flesh, He who came to heal the sick, to befriend the outcast, and to forgive the sinner. His gentle presence reminds us that grace is never distant or out of reach; it dwells deeply within each act of kindness, each moment of mercy offered to another. When we help a friend in need, when we share a kind word or a gentle smile, we become vessels of that grace. It flows through our actions like a river, touching lives and hearts beyond what we can see or imagine.

Grace does not ignore our struggles or pretend that life is always easy. In fact, it is in the midst of our trials and failures that grace shines the brightest, like a candle flickering warmly against the dark. It gives us courage to face the hard days with hope, to hold fast to kindness even when it feels difficult, and to trust that God's love is stronger than any fear or sorrow. This beautiful gift teaches us patience, for ourselves and for others, even when mistakes are made and forgiveness seems hard to offer. Grace is not just a word or a promise; it is the very breath of life that sustains us, a gentle power guiding us to live with hearts full of love and hands ready to serve.

As children grow and discover the world around them, grace becomes their companion and guide, helping them learn that nobody is perfect, and that is perfectly alright. Every child will sometimes feel afraid, sad, or overwhelmed by the mistakes they make or the challenges they face, but grace is the reminder that they are always deeply loved by God, who sees their hearts and knows their worth. It teaches kindness not only outwardly but also inwardly, nurturing a gentle voice within that encourages forgiveness and hope, rather than hurt or despair. Through grace, every fall is a chance to rise again, every tear a seed for joy, and every moment of sadness a doorway to compassion. It calls children to live with open hearts, ready to give and receive love, wrapped always in the safety of God's embrace.

Forgiveness grows directly from grace, intertwining like the vines of a sturdy tree. When God's grace fills our hearts, it overflows into forgiveness, both of others and ourselves. Forgiveness is a gift we give to free our spirits and to allow love to bloom even after hurt. Sometimes, when friends or family make mistakes or say unkind words, hurt feelings can grow like thorns, tightening around the heart and making it hard to feel joy or peace. Yet grace encourages us to see beyond those thorns, to remember the goodness that still grows within every person, and to offer forgiveness as a way to restore harmony and love. It is a gentle gift that invites us to let go of anger and bitterness and to choose the path of kindness and understanding. Just as God's grace covers our imperfections, so too can our forgiveness cover the wounds caused by others, bringing healing and hope to every broken place.

Grace also calls us to grow, not just taller or stronger in body, but richer and deeper in spirit. It is the sunlight and rain for the seeds planted in our souls, encouraging faith to blossom and kindness to take root in every action we take. As children embrace grace, they become part of a beautiful circle of love, where faith is nurtured not by worry or fear, but by the joyous knowledge that God's love never ends. This growth is not quick or easy, but it is steady and sure, like a tree reaching slowly toward the sky, its branches spreading wide to shelter and protect. Through prayers, through learning scripture, and through loving one another, grace becomes the foundation upon which children build their lives. It gives them the strength to face the world with courage, to hold tightly to hope, and to share God's light with those around them.

Sometimes, the idea of grace can seem so big and beautiful that it feels almost too wonderful to be true. Yet it is very real, a promise that God makes to each child and to all people: that no matter how many times we falter, His love will always be there to lift us up, to welcome us home, and to help us walk forward with joy. It teaches us that we do not travel alone, that God journeys beside us, guiding us gently with His word and His Spirit. This truth is a comfort in every season of life, a steady anchor in times of change and uncertainty. By holding tight to grace, children learn that they too can be lights in the world, shining with kindness, patience, and love that comes straight from God's heart.

In the quiet moments before sleep, or when the sun sets in colors of gold and crimson, it is good to remember grace's gentle song, a melody of hope and peace that fills the soul with calm and joy. It calls us to be thankful, to see each day as a precious gift, and to live with hearts open wide to the wonders of God's love. With grace as a guide, children can walk confidently on their path, knowing that each step is watched over and blessed. They can carry this gift into the playground, the classroom, and the home, sharing the light of God's mercy softly with friends and family alike.

Grace is not only a gift to receive but also a treasure to give away. When children learn to live with grace, they learn to be gentle in their words, generous in their hearts, and forgiving in their spirits. These gifts create ripples, spreading far beyond what any one child can see. A kind word spoken in grace may brighten a lonely day; a forgiving heart may heal a hurt that seemed impossible. In this way, grace multiplies, growing like a garden full of blooming flowers, each petal a testament to God's enduring love. Every act of kindness, every prayer of gratitude, every choice to forgive is a seed planted for a future full of hope and peace.

So let us carry grace as a precious gift, a light that brightens our days and warms our hearts. Let it remind us that no matter what happens, we are loved beyond measure and are called to love one another with the same tenderness and care. Grace is the story's beautiful ending and the wonderful beginning of each new day. With grace, we are never alone, never forgotten, and always held close in the arms of God's infinite love. Let this gift inspire us to live with thankful hearts, to grow in kindness, and to share the joy of salvation with all who cross our paths. This is the greatest treasure, the most radiant seed of all, the gift of grace, given freely and forever.

Sharing Grace

In the gentle light of a new day, when the sun's first rays spill softly through the windowpanes, there lies a precious opportunity, the golden chance to share grace with the world around us. Grace is like a tender seed planted deep within the heart; it grows quietly, unseen by many, but it blossoms beautifully when touched by love and kindness. To share grace is to open our hands and hearts to others, offering them understanding and forgiveness even when it is not asked for. It is a gentle whisper that says, "I see you, I care for you, and I am here for you," even when words may seem small or actions might appear simple. This kindness, wrapped in the warmth of grace, becomes a bridge over troubled waters, bringing peace where there once was strife, and light where darkness lingered.

Children, you may wonder how you can share such a mighty gift as grace every day, especially when the world sometimes feels hurried and busy. Yet, the essence of grace lies not in grand gestures or mighty deeds but in the choice to love, forgive, and show mercy whenever and wherever you can. Imagine a friend who has made a mistake; instead of frowning or turning away, you choose to smile and listen, telling them with your eyes and actions that nobody is perfect and that forgiveness is as wide and as deep as the ocean. That moment of choosing love over anger, patience over impatience, is a seed of grace planted firmly in the soil of friendship. It is in these ordinary moments, when you comfort a sibling, help a classmate, or speak softly to someone who is sad, that grace takes root and flourishes.

To share grace means to understand that everyone is on a journey, some walking through sunshine and laughter, others trudging through shadows and tears. Just as the Bible teaches us through the stories of Jesus, showing grace to others is not about waiting for them to be perfect, but loving them just as they are, with all their flaws and stumbles. The Savior's tender heart reached out to the lonely, the tired, and the lost, embracing them without condition. Following His example, even the smallest among us can radiate that same grace to our family, neighbors, and friends. When you choose to give a kind word, hold a forgiving heart, or carry a humble spirit, you are echoing the great love of God, making the sacred language of the King James Bible come alive within your own life.

Sometimes sharing grace asks us to be brave. Forgiveness can feel as towering as a mountain when someone has hurt us deeply or when we face unkindness ourselves. Yet, grace whispers softly that forgiveness is a gift we give not only to others but to ourselves, freeing our hearts from bitterness and sadness. When a young child chooses to forgive a hurtful word spoken by a friend, they learn a profound truth: peace grows not from holding anger tightly, but from releasing it gently into the hands of God. In that moment, the spirit of grace softly wraps around their soul, teaching them that love is stronger than pain, and hope brighter than despair. Forgiveness does not erase the past, but it paints new beginnings in the colors of mercy and fresh joy.

Sharing grace also means seeing the good in others, even when it hides behind difficult moments or mistakes. Often, children and grown-ups alike make choices that lead their hearts away from kindness, but grace shines its light on the beautiful possibilities that dwell within each person. When you notice a classmate feeling lonely, a family member struggling with sadness, or even a stranger who seems lost, your gracious heart can offer a smile, a helping hand, or a quiet word of encouragement. These actions, though they may seem small, ripple outward like gentle waves across a calm sea, touching lives in ways you may never fully know. Each moment where grace is shared becomes a sacred thread weaving people together in a tapestry of hope and love.

The beauty of grace is that it never runs out. It is an inexhaustible stream flowing from the heart of God, always ready to pour into your life and to flow through you to others. When you find your own heart full of grace, you become a vessel of God's love, a beacon in your home, school, and community. You may share grace by patiently listening to a story that needs no fixing, by saying "I'm sorry" honestly when you make a mistake, by helping someone silently in need without expecting thanks, or by quietly praying for those who hurt. Each graceful act is a soft light in a shadowed world, reminding everyone that kindness and forgiveness are mighty forces for good.

As you grow, you will discover that sharing grace is not always easy, but it is always worth it. There may be days when your patience is thin, your heart feels heavy, and forgiving seems impossible. In those moments, remember that grace is not something you must conjure from your own strength alone. By turning your eyes heavenward, you can ask God for help to love as Jesus loved, to forgive as He forgave, and to be kind even when it is hard. The gentle language of the King James Bible reminds us, "Be ye kind one to another, tenderhearted, forgiving one another, even as God for Christ's sake hath forgiven you." This sacred call is not just for grown-ups but for you, too, a loving invitation to let grace be your guiding light.

Each day brings new opportunities, many wrapped in simple moments, to show grace in action. When you listen carefully to someone's story without interrupting, you open a door for grace to enter. When you share your toys or your time without expecting anything in return, you pour out God's kindness into the world. When you forgive a friend who has hurt your feelings, you embrace the promise of salvation that tells us all can be made new. These daily acts, woven together, create a lifelong pattern of grace that grows stronger with each choice, each smile, each gentle touch.

And so, dear children, as you close these pages and step back into your world, carry with you the tender hope that grace is not just a word found in books but a living gift to be scattered like seeds in the garden of your life. Plant grace in your words and actions, nourish it with love and patience, and watch as it blooms into kindness that blesses everyone you meet. In sharing grace, you participate in the sacred story that began in the Garden of Eden and continues through the life of Jesus Christ, a story of love, forgiveness, and eternal hope.

May your hearts always be open, your hands always ready to help, and your spirits forever filled with the gentle strength of grace. In embracing grace, you will find a path to joy, healing, and a love that knows no end. And as you grow in faith, remember: the greatest gift you can ever give is the grace that mirrors God's own great love for you.

Living in God's Love

To live in God's love is to walk in a garden that never fades, where the flowers of kindness bloom eternally, and the gentle breeze whispers peace upon every heart. Imagine, dear child, that each day you arise, wrapped in the tender arms of the Almighty, His love enfolding you as a cloak woven of light and mercy. There is no place too dark, no moment too fearful, where His grace cannot reach; His hand is ever extended, ready to catch you when you stumble and to lift you when you fall. This love is not like the fleeting kindness of summer's sun, which warms only for a season, but rather it is the steadfast light of the morning star, shining unwaveringly through the veil of clouds, guiding your feet along paths of truth and goodness. To live in God's care is to know that each breath you draw is a gift wrapped in infinite compassion, fashioned by the Creator who calls you His cherished child.

When you open your heart to this divine embrace, you begin to see the world through eyes that know forgiveness is the key that unlocks freedom and peace. Therein lies a secret, whispered softly in the quiet moments of prayer, that no mistake is too great to be mended, no sorrow too deep to be healed. God's love is a balm that soothes the aching soul, reminding you that though you may sometimes drift away, His grace yearns to bring you back with open arms and boundless mercy. Living in His love means carrying this truth gently within you, allowing it to soften your thoughts and temper your actions. It is in this tender transformation that you find the strength to forgive others as you have been forgiven, to speak kindly where harsh words might have flourished, and to extend a hand of friendship to those who feel alone or forgotten.

The journey you have traveled, from the dawn of creation's innocence to the radiant promise of redemption, has shown you that God's love is the light that dissolves the shadows of sin and despair. Each story you have heard, each lesson learned in the cadence of ancient scriptures, plants a seed of grace deep within your soul, a seed that grows and blossoms as you choose love over fear, hope over doubt. To live confidently in God's care is to know, even when storms gather and the way seems uncertain, that a refuge is always within reach. Like the child who trusts the sheltering arms of a parent amid thunder and rain, so you may find peace knowing that God's steadfast presence encircles you like a fortress of light.

Embracing grace means that your heart becomes a garden rich with joy, blooming with every act of kindness, every word of forgiveness spoken. It is a place where love flows freely, spilling over to touch the lives of others in ways both great and small. When you give love, dear child, you become a reflection of the Savior's own heart, a beacon drawing others toward the warmth of Heaven's promises. In this way, each step you take within God's care fills the earth with hope, a hope that blossoms in the eyes of a friend who feels seen, in the smile of a neighbor who feels understood, in the gentle hand you hold when sorrow visits. To live confidently in His love is to join a dance of grace that never ends, weaving together the hearts of all who dare to trust in mercy's song.

Yet to live in God's love is no mere comfort without purpose; it calls you to be a guardian of that love, to share its light with the world earnestly. It beckons you to become a shepherd who tends not only their own soul but watches carefully over the fragile hearts around them. In your playgrounds, in your schools, and in the quiet moments at home, your kind deeds are like ripples upon a still lake, spreading far beyond what eyes can see. Each smile you offer, each gentle word you choose, each moment you bear patience with those who falter is a living testimony to the grace that dwells within. Remember that even the smallest acts of love are mighty in the eyes of God, for they carry the fragrance of Heaven itself.

When doubts arise, as they surely will when the world's troubles seem heavy upon your shoulders, remember the words spoken through ages past, drawn from the wellspring of the King James Bible: "Fear thou not; for I am with thee: be not dismayed; for I am thy God." This promise is not unlike a lantern carried steadfastly through the night, casting away the shadows of loneliness, worry, or fear. In your moments of uncertainty, whisper this truth softly to your heart, and feel the calm that it brings, like the still waters that restore a weary soul. God's love is your anchor and your sails, steadying you amid the waves while also urging you onward toward the harbor of peace.

Living in God's love also means growing in faith as a tender plant stretches toward the sun, reaching ever upward, seeking to bloom more fully with each new day. Faith is not a distant, dusty thing hidden in lofty towers, but a warm companion who walks beside you, holding your hand through joys and trials alike. It is a voice that sings the song of hope in your heart and paints your world with the colors of promise, even when skies turn gray. To walk with faith is to trust in what you cannot see but know deep within, a trust nurtured from the stories you have learned, and the gentle presence that never forsakes you. Faith leads you to see that grace is a seed ready to grow, that kindness is a stream flowing from the heart of God, and that your life is a precious vessel brimming with the light of salvation.

As you live each day wrapped in God's loving care, you begin to understand that you are never truly alone. Just as the stars in the night sky are countless and steadfast, so too is God's presence vast and unceasing. When you feel small or afraid, remember that the Creator of all things artfully formed each star, each flower, and every heartbeat with tender intention. You are a masterpiece of divine love, carefully crafted with purpose and hope. To live confidently in this truth is to carry a joy that nothing can take away, a joy that lifts your spirit and encourages you to share with others the gift you have received. Your life becomes a living hymn of praise, a song written in the language of kindness, forgiveness, and grace.

There will be moments when the path seems steep, and the burdens of sadness or disappointment weigh heavily upon your shoulders. Yet even in those times, God's love remains a steadfast refuge, a treasure hidden not in distant lands, but within your very soul. The Spirit of God whispers to you in the silence, comforting and guiding, reminding you that no sorrow is final, no mistake is beyond forgiveness, no heart is beyond healing. To live in His love is not to be perfect, but to be perfectly loved despite imperfection. It is to rest in the assurance that your worth is not earned by deeds alone but granted by a love that never ceases, a love that never fails.

In this great love, you find the courage to be yourself, to show the world your true heart shining with goodness and grace. It frees you from the fear of being judged or cast aside and fills you with the boldness to walk humbly, yet confidently, knowing your name is written in the Book of Life. As you grow in this understanding, may your days be marked by gentle compassion and unwavering hope, like a tree planted by the rivers of water, whose leaf shall not wither. Each act of love you perform waters this tree, causing it to flourish and bear fruit for the blessing of many.

Dear child, as you move forward from this journey of discovering sin and salvation, remember this: the seeds of grace that have been planted in your heart will one day bloom into mighty oaks of faith and love, sheltering not just yourself but all who come after you. The story of your life is a beautiful chapter in God's grand design, written not with ink alone, but with deeds borne of a heart overflowing with divine love. As you live confidently in His care, may you always wear the gentle crown of kindness, walk in the quiet strength of forgiveness, and shine with the everlasting light of grace, that all who meet you may glimpse a reflection of Heaven itself.